THE ORION BOOK OF THE WRITTEN WORD

THE ORION PRESS, *New York*

THE ORION BOOK OF the written word

by Etiemble

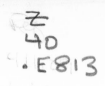

"But, when a Phoenician (he was, I imagine, some tradesman, without title or birth) had taught men how to paint the spoken word and capture the fugitive voice with a few strokes, a vague uneasiness began to be felt by those who were getting tired of working for others; and at the same time there developed a monarchic dedication among those who insisted at all costs that others work for them. The first written words were liberty, law, right, justice, reason; and from then on, it became increasingly evident that this ingenious art would continue to chip away at privileges and emoluments. From that time may be dated the anxieties of men in high places, the courtiers."

Paul-Louis Courier
Letter of March 10, 1820,
to the editor of the
periodical, Censeur.

"Ts'ang Kie* cried during the night: he really had something to cry about."

Sad song for Wou Ki-tseu
from Wou Wei-ye (1609-1671).

*Ts'ang Kie, legendary inventor of writing.

I have just run the waxed point of my brand-new pen through a flame to ready it for writing this book about writing. In 1961 of the Christian era—and for me to whom writing is something of a profession—what can be more natural than this activity? I am even unconscious of writer's cramp. For ten hours running, if necessary, I can write without fatigue in this cursive scrawl which will present me with an undecipherable scribble if I merely turn my paper upside down. It is easy to imagine that writing always existed; yet, men have lived and died for perhaps a million years but have actually been writing for only about six thousand of them.

As if trying to recapture the time lost by our ancestors, the postman every morning brings me handwritten, typed, or printed letters from all over the world, and I am not counting mimeographed circulars, prospectuses, newspapers, periodicals, books, and still more books. Sometimes, I reflect on the sheer volume of the words written or printed every single day and try to calculate the quantity of timber felled daily for the manufacture of all this paper. Overshadowed, in this respect, is the performance of Gargantua's horse who, while trying to rid himself of flies as he was crossing a forest, lashed his tail so vigorously that he cut down the woods with it and made the great French plain which we call la Beauce. Surrounded as I am by these millions of volumes when I wander among the bookshelves of a large library, how should I not feel crushed by the mass of written material? Sometimes, disheartened, I burn a pound or two of my literary attempts or, better still, give away a carton or two of my books. The press depresses me; print oppresses me. To reassure

me, they tell me that this civilization of the written word, my civilization, is dying; that radio, television, and magnetic tapes—in brief, what jargon calls the audio-visual media—are heralding the end of alphabets and ideograms.

Actually, is writing an evil or a boon? Was Court de Gébelin wrong when he praised it in this way two centuries ago?: "...this Art which speaks to the eye, which paints for the sight what sound expresses to the mind through the medium of the ear, which is as fixed as the voice is fugitive, which will continue to exist centuries after those who created it will have descended into the night of their tombs, this Art which perpetuates the Sciences, which facilitates their acquisition, which permits past cultures to help perfect those of the present time—all of which will serve together as the foundation for the immense edifice which future times will fashion."

In a sense, yes, he was wrong. But, according to Paul-Louis Courier in his preface to *Hérodote*, "When writing came into being, there were those who disapproved of this invention which was not yet justified in the eyes of many people; they thought it would diminish the power of the memory and make the mind lazy." As for me, I often curse this art which, by substituting vision for hearing, diverts Americans from mental arithmetic, corrupts all poetry, and, infinitely multiplying the falsehoods of the powerful, submits man—and not only the Mussulman—to a *mektoub,* or common fate: "It's so, I tell ya, 'cause I seen it in the newspaper!" When I recall a

Coffer of Chapenapit. Bronze incrusted with gold and silver. Twenty-fifth Dynasty.

detail of *Tristes Tropiques* (there is an illiterate Indian who pretends to know how to write in order to enslave those whom he had up to then treated as equals), why should I not feel uneasy, belonging to a civilization in which writing became the tongue of Aesop: the best thing, and, as we see, also the worst? Ah, yes, we must not forget the *Antigone* of Sophocles. To the written laws, hardened into codes, congealed in their procedures, frozen by the pomp and paraphernalia of the magistracy, this pure young girl opposes the unwritten laws, those for which every human being worthy of the name ought to sacrifice his liberty, even his life, whenever there is conflict between these and those others. If the man who does not reflect, but who governs, invokes the tablets of the law as if they were divine commandments, why cannot the woman who does not govern, but who reflects, reveal, because she understands everything, that these written laws are obstacles to the progress of morality?

Perhaps Gourmont is agreeably mistaken when he conceives the intrusion of writing as marking the end of the time when woman incarnated the archives of the human race: "Standing up as narrator, before the Creator, woman founded a repertory, a library, archives. The first songbook was the memory of a woman; and, likewise, the first collection of tales, the first file of documents.

"Still, the invention of writing, like all successive manifestations of progress, did diminish the archival importance of woman. Since everything deemed worthy of remembrance was being preserved on durable materials by means of signs, woman gave herself the trouble and the pleasure of keeping alive what man condemned to oblivion." Hence, to the "conserving genius of woman," we owe oral literature, "the themes of which surpass in number those of written literature."

Whether we consider it the worst or the best of things, writing, in either case, merits our consideration.

"If the problem of the origin of language does not admit of any satisfactory solution, this is not true of the problem of writing." (Joseph Vendryès.) Nevertheless, it should be stated plainly that even though we have at our command very scholarly histories in several languages on the subject of writing—in France, for instance, those of James Février or of Marcel Cohen—we do not really know why man first began to write. Court de Gébelin thought that writing could have appeared only among agricultural peoples: it would have been indispensable for them to keep an account of their workers, their herds, their fields, their earnings and expenses. According to Father Wieger of the Society of Jesuits, "writing was first an instrument of government, of administration." In fact, at least one text confirms this idea in China: *"Chang-kou hien-jen kie cheng yi tcheu."* This means: "The holy men of very ancient times knotted strings [wrote] in order to govern." To this practical interpretation, probably of Confucianist inspiration, Jacques Gernet opposes another and wonders whether "from its earliest usage, writing in China had not been exclusively a means of communication with the gods or at least certain categories of divinities."

Scribe. Detail of the Mastaba of Akhethetep. Sakkara. Fifth Dynasty.

But if we want to know, really know, 10
whether writing was invented once and for all
by one civilization, or whether on several
occasions in the course of history several human communities conceived the same idea,
general opinion, until recent times, attributed
to China and Egypt, respectively, the honor of
having perfected at about the same time the
ideogram and the hieroglyph. Still, it appears
that this supposition was unacceptable to various apologists in the eighteenth century who
squandered treasures of intelligence explain-
ing that ideograms are derived from hieroglyphics. Take the Chinese word which signifies a boat: *tchouan* 船; this breaks down
as: boat 舟 + eight 八 + mouth 口. Now, what
famous ship sheltered eight people? Noah's
Ark, of course! From this it is deduced that
the Noachites transmitted to the Chinese the
secret of writing invented on the shores of
the Mediterranean! For other reasons, somewhat less poetic, Bottéro is inclined to think—
and he is not alone—that the invention of
writing, like all the great discoveries, occurred
only once on our planet. It made such an
obvious impression that it spread east and
west in that epoch and from that region in
which, during the fourth millennium before
our reckoning, it was created by the civilization which we call the Sumerian. The history
of writing, then, and, consequently, history
itself, began in Sumer.

Such prestige do men attach to written characters—after six millenniums—that many civilizations claim to have received them from
the gods, and they attribute magical values to

Cuneiform writing.

them. When certain reformers in the twentieth century wanted to revise Arabic writing, which is so complicated, with four forms for each letter, according to whether it stands alone or people scrupulously carried every scrap of paper upon which they could discern even the washed-out trace of an ancient character—multiplied aberrant characters that nobody

Seal of a Sumerian "obstetrician." Twenty-second century B.C.

in initial, middle, or final position; and which is so incomplete, on the other hand, that it ignores capital letters—what an outcry burst forth! Change the way of writing that Allah himself had revealed to men! Even if capital letters might be accepted, nobody up to now has been able to effect the reduction of the four forms for each letter to one.

The same superstitious respect for anything written—which produced in China those "shrines for written characters" to which

dares to correct, like 說 *chouo,* to speak, with the meaning of 悅 *yue,* to rejoice, because an absent-minded scribe once copied *chouo* 說 for *yue* 悅.

Those Congolese messengers who pierce with the thrust of a spear the letter they are charged to deliver react to anything written almost as those good people of my childhood used to do when they saw the prescription—to them cabalistic—of the physician and believed themselves cured because they under-

fi

stood nothing of the scrawled pothooks of the "doctor," their shaman, or medicine man.

It is not surprising that the Egyptians also

*Aegean hieroglyphic script. Discus
of Phaestos. Crete. Second millennium* B.C.

saw in their god, Thot, the father of writing; that the Cretans were grateful to Zeus for theirs; that the Jews rendered thanks to Yahweh—to the *divine writing* of *Exodus*, XXI, 18, *Isaiah*, VIII, 1, opposes a *human writing*—and that the Japanese imagined they

had received, before the Chinese characters, what they called the writing of the gods, *kami-yo no moji*. It amuses me that in these presumably divine signs, scholars have subsequently identified a bastardization of Korean characters. Man is so modest that he sometimes attributes to superhuman powers manifestations of his own triumph over his animal nature.

It is remarkable to observe how man, several thousand years after the invention of written characters, remains convinced of the magical virtues of any alphabet whatsoever. In his *In Praise of Folly*, Erasmus portrays an octogenarian infatuated with theology to the point of demonstrating "with a marvelous subtlety" that everything that can be said about Jesus "is hidden in the letters of his name." Indeed, the octogenarian said, the name of Jesus in Latin has only three cases, which obviously means the three beings of the Holy Trinity. Observe further that the nominative ends in S, JesuS; the accusative in M, JesuM; and the ablative in U, JesU. Now, these three endings, S. M. U., conceal an ineffable mystery; because they are the first letters of the three Latin words—*Summum* (zenith), *Medium* (center), and *Ultimum* (nadir), they clearly signify that Jesus is the beginning, the middle, and the end of all things. A mystery rather more difficult than all this remained to be explained, but our doctor acquitted himself in a completely mathematical manner. He divided the word Jesus into two equal parts so that the letter S stood by itself in the middle. This letter S, he went on to say, which we remove from the name of Jesus, is called Syn among the Hebrews. Now, *syn* is a Scotch word which, I believe, means *sin*. This surely

13 shows us, as clear as the day, that it is Jesus who removed sin from the world.

From an article by Dupont-Sommer, we also learn that some Gnostic had so ingeniously expounded the letter *Vav*, which figures in the spelling of Yahweh in Hebrew, that in the end this *Vav* was equivalent to Jesus. Likewise, in the Indian world, what zeal we find in the elucidation of the writing of *aum*, the syllable of syllables, "in which the voice, passing from the most open vowel to the most closed consonant, traverses at one sweep the entire cycle of sounds or, rather, occupies its center!" (Lanza del Vasto.) Who is so blind as not to see that the *A* denotes *Asti*, existence; the *U*, *Utpatti*, birth; the *M*, *Mrtyu*, death? Etc., etc.

Why should I be astonished? After all, a month ago, I discovered in the *Shilappadikaram* that the *panchatantra*, the sacred Word of Jainism: *a-si-a-u-sa*, embodies the five *parameshthin*—A(rhat), Si(ddha), A(charya), U(padhyada), and Sa(dhu). Should I then be surprised to learn that the twelve signs of the zodiac correspond to the twenty-four letters of the Greek alphabet and that the seven planets correspond to the seven vowels of this same alphabet: αεηιουω? If in the capital letter upsilon, Υ, the Christians no longer discerned a planet, but the crossroad where man must choose, like Hercules of old, between vice and virtue; and if the capital letter tau, T, presented itself to them as the image of the true cross, we should not be amazed.

These are the kinds of transformations which can be evoked by anyone who loses

Punic stele. About third century B.C.

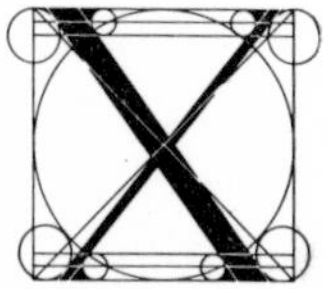

ΑΣΙΝΗ ΦΑΝΕΡΟΝ ΤΟΙΣ ΕΥΕΡΓ
ΝΟΙΣ ΑΥΤΟΝ ΟΤΙ ΠΡΟΑΙΡΕΤΑΙ Χ
ΑΠΟΔΙΔΟΝΑΙ ΕΠΑΙΝΕΣΑΙ ΜΕ
ΑΡΕΤΗΣ ΕΝΕΚΕΝ ΚΑΙ ΕΥΝΟΙΑ
ΤΕΛΕΙ ΠΕΡΙ ΤΟΝ ΔΗΜΟΝ ΣΤΗ
ΕΙΚΟΝΑ ΧΑΛΚΗΝ ΕΝ ΤΗΙ ΑΓΟ
ΝΟ ΑΝΑΘΗΣΕΤΑΙ ΑΓΟΛΕ
ΟΣ ΤΑΙ ΑΙΟΡΟΣ ΔΑΝΗΕΙΚΩΝ
ΑΧΕΙΕΛΕΣΘΑ ΠΟ ΝΙ ΠΟΛΙΤ
ΔΥΟΟ ΙΤΙΝΕΣ ΕΙΔ Ο Σ ΟΝ ΤΑ
ΠΙΜΕΛΗΣ ΟΝΤΑΙ ΟΓΟ Σ ΣΥΝ
ΤΗ ΠΛΑΣΙ ΙΗ ΤΗΣ ΕΙΚΟΝΟ
ΟΣ ΤΑΜΙΑΣ ΙΑ ΧΜΑΣ ΤΕ
ΑΠΟ ΓΑΤΟΝ ΧΡΗΜΑΤΩΝ ΟΙΕ
ΤΑΙ ΓΟΡΟΝ ΣΥΝΤΑΞΑΝΤΕ
Ι ΤΑΜΙΑΙ ΟΛ ΤΑΜΙΑΣ ΛΟΓ Τ
ΤΑΙ ΚΑΘ ΟΦΑΝΤΗ ΓΙ ΛΟΣΙΝ Π
ΠΙΜΕΛΗΤΑΙ ΕΛΕΣΘΑΙ ΔΕ ΚΑΙ
ΝΤΕΟΥ ΤΙΝΕΣ ΑΦΙΚΟΜΕΝΟΙ Τ

himself in reflection on the alphabet. "The weak-minded, applying themselves to *thinking* about the first letter of the alphabet can be quickly hurled into madness!" (Rimbaud.) Consider Claudel, Rimbaud's disciple: in the S of the German *Spitzschrift,* 𝔙, he most cleverly identified the symbol of the verb "to see," *sehen,* in German, as an outline of a face, to which it was only necessary to add two eyes: 𝔙. Nor am I forgetting the "gematrical" speculations of the Greek world, thanks to which the letters in Nero (Νέρων) translated with the help of the appropriate numerical coefficients into numbers, are equivalent to 1005; just as from the sentence, ἰδίαν μητέρα ἀπέκτεινε (he killed his own mother), the interpretation follows that Νέρων had to kill his own mother, unless he was given the name of Νέρων because he was going to murder her! And only recently in the United States, there was an attempt to read into the letters of the word *nylon* the proof that this fiber was going to ruin the Japanese economy. NYLON = N [ow] Y [ou] L [ousy] O [ld] N [ipponese].

Writing, then, has only exasperated this tendency of man to hold the word sacred. Very well, let us accept this much. But as a creative force, it is energetically mocked in Kabir's *Cabaret de l'amour:*

Si en répétant "Râm," le monde est sauvé,
Alors, en disant "sucre," la bouche est sucrée.

(If, by repeating "Râm," the world is saved,
Then, by saying "sugar," the mouth is
   sweetened.)

Greek inscription. Theangela.
Third century B.C.

It is as if our phonetic alphabets had to be burdened with "abstract speculations" because, thanks to what Février calls "choc en retour" (a retroactive shock), they replaced an ideog-

Trajan's inscription. Trajan's Column.
Second century.

raphy itself laden with souvenirs of magic.

Let this brief excursion into the torments of writing suffice. To pursue it further would entail the risk of my demoralizing you and of ridding myself of the desire to dip my pen into the ink again, whether it be a square-nibbed pen or a quill.

Let us rather ask whom we ought to admire more, those who designed the first pictographs, then the first cuneiforms, then the first alphabets, or those who, in the nineteenth and twentieth centuries, succeeded in deciphering hieroglyphics, cuneiforms, Cretan Linear B and Cypriote syllabaries, Ugaritic alphabets, and so on, nearly all of those scripts which, through-

*Small plaque of inscribed wood
from Easter Island, called "talking wood."*

out the millenniums, had remained impenetrable to us.

In spite of the celebrated principle: "Any text composed in a known language and in an unknown script will be deciphered sooner or later," deciphering is not always easy. Any reader of Poe, any officer at military headquarters knows the principles of simple decoding: to decode the simple transposition of an alphabetical language, it is sufficient to know the relative frequency of each vowel and consonant, the usual grouping of letters, and the principal endings.

But in a system of writing like that of the Mayas, in which phoneticism plays hardly any role, this rule is not worth much. Besides, if there is the slightest possibility that the decipherer does not know either the principles or the language which the writing is supposed to transcribe, the difficulties may appear insurmountable. For instance, in the first edition of his *Histoire de l'écriture*, Février stated that nobody would ever "really" be able to read the Cretan script. But in 1953, that is, five years later, Ventris and Chadwick, two young Englishmen, published their now-famous twenty pages: *Evidence for Greek Dialect in the Mycenean Archives*. After various fruitless attempts, Ventris presupposed that the Creto-Mycenean Linear B script had a connection with the Greek language. Then, all he needed to do was to apply the simple principles of cryptography to discover some signs which could correspond to the archaic genitive in *-oio*, that of Homer. Since Ventris was not a Hellenist, he associated himself with Chadwick; and before the accidental death of the former in 1956, both men worked very well together on their common enterprise. In 1953, Blegen confirmed their readings; and somewhat later, Allan Wace praised them in these terms: "In the course of his brief life, Ventris attained immortality by deciphering the Mycenean B script and discovering in it the most ancient form known to us of the Greek lan-

*Madagascan "magic" handwriting.
Seventeenth century.*

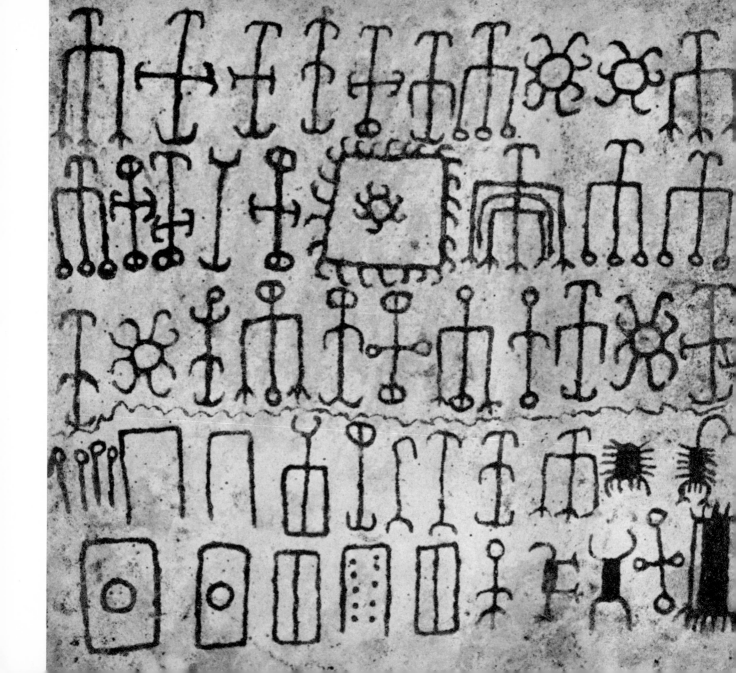

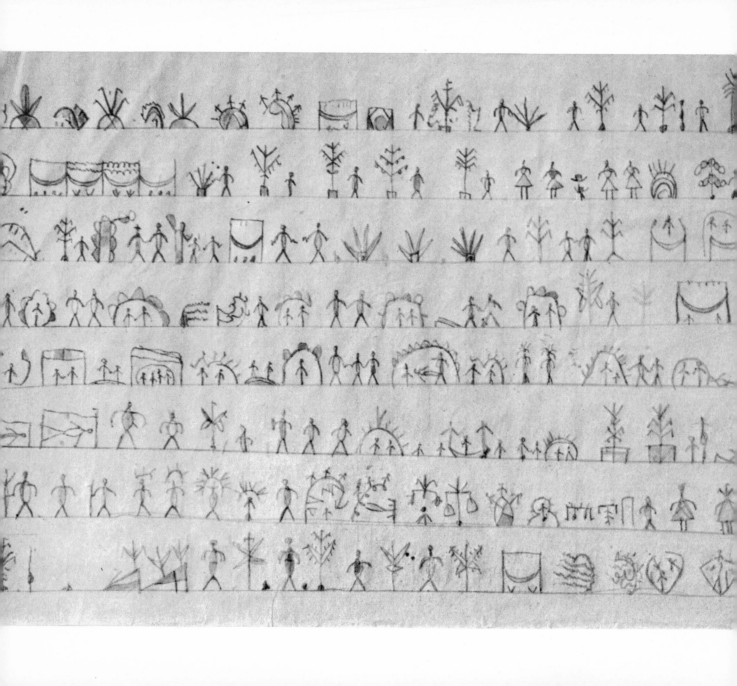

guage, that which was spoken seven hundred years before Homer."

To judge by the extravagances of the *Oedipus Aegiptiacus,* in which the Jesuit Kircher had, nevertheless, a presentiment of the relationship between Coptic and the hieroglyphics, it was folly to dream of deciphering the Egyptian inscriptions. Yet, here is where Champollion stepped in. While Kircher had insisted upon considering each hieroglyph as the symbol of one object and one idea, Champollion rediscovered through reasoning power the intuitive idea already formulated by Guignes and Carsten Niebuhr which they, however, had been unable to bring to fruition. He deduced from the Rosetta Stone, the Greek version of which contains 486 words as against 1,419 hieroglyphic signs, that Egyptian writing, assuming that it notated some words, ought surely to notate letters also. Whereas Thomas Young, in 1814, had only an imperfect notion about the reading of the cartouches of Berenice and of Ptolemy, Champollion, as early as 1821, knew how to read the Pharaoh's name correctly as *Ptolmjs,* instead of the *Ptolemaios* of Young. On September 14, 1882, he ran to L'Institut, shouted: "I've got it!" and fainted. Thirteen days later, there appeared his *Lettre à Monsieur Dacier* about the alphabet of Egyptian hieroglyphics. Exhausted by overwork and consumed by his genius, when Champollion died ten years later, he had founded Egyptology and established a method for deciphering unknown scripts. No one can usurp his glory.

Pictograph of the Couna Indians in Panama: Songs to reach the soul of an invalid.

The decipherers of such ancient scripts as the Cypriote syllabary or the Giblite inscriptions of Byblos seem admirable, indeed, to us, but one of the most meritorious works of that

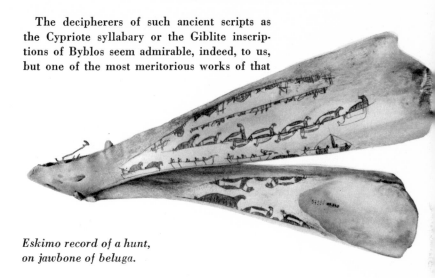

Eskimo record of a hunt, on jawbone of beluga.

time is probably the achievement of all those scholars whose complex of courage, intelligence, and sometimes madness compelled the cuneiform inscriptions to reveal, bit by bit, their laws and relationships. From Chardin, who brought back with him from his voyage to Persia the first document on cuneiform characters, to the recent book of S. N. Kramer, *History Begins in Sumer,* what progress there has been, and what difficulties and disputes! But this is routine! Stimulated by Chardin, Kämpfer, and others, Carsten Niebuhr (1733-1815) was able to distinguish in the inscriptions of Darius and Xerxes three different scripts and then set up for them an alphabet of forty-two signs, thirty-two of them accurate. Afterwards, various scholars worked on Persepolitan cuneiform inscriptions. And then, before the inaccessible Rock of Behistun (more correctly, Bisutun) stood the Englishman,

Rawlinson. But he refused to be beaten. In 1839, he translated two hundred lines of the cliff inscription and revealed to the scholarly world that Old Persian cuneiform is an alphabetical consonantal script with traces of syllabism. Another Englishman, William H. Fox Talbot (1800-1877), made possible the decipherment of the Akkadian cuneiform script. In 1857, the text of the same Assyrian inscription, unknown to all four of them, was submitted to four scholars: Rawlinson and Fox Talbot, joined by Hincks and the German Jewish scholar, Julius Oppert. The four versions agreed with one another. From that day forward, the decipherment of Akkadian cuneiforms was considered accomplished.

Whereas Champollion was able to understand the hieroglyphics all by himself, the fraternal collaboration of all kinds of savants was necessary to bring about the solution of cuneiforms because, as more became known about this kind of writing, and as it became necessary to delve deeply into a more and more remote past, the difficulties could only multiply. They could multiply to the point of madness, in the precise sense of the word: after having deciphered the text of a tablet which he had discovered in an ancient limestone layer, and having exclaimed ecstatically, "After two thousand years of oblivion, I am the first to read this text!" George Smith, one of the glories of the British Museum, tried to strip off his clothing! He was to die quite young, at thirty-six.

If one excepts the luck which permitted Bossert to discover, but only in 1947, the bilingual inscriptions of Karatepe in hieroglyphic Hittite and Phoenician, it is the genius and patience of men which have solved the principal problems of cuneiform writing. We owe to Rawlinson the discovery of polyphony; to Jensen, the decipherment of the name of the city of Karkhemish, in hieroglyphic Hittite; to Hrozny, the interpretation of the tablets of Boghazkeui, from which there emerged in 1915 his work on the language of the Hittites. By degrees, cuneiform writing sent researchers farther and farther back to Sumer, its existence unsuspected until not so long ago, since Maspero did not say a word about it in his *Histoire ancienne des peuples de l'Orient classique,* an ancient history of the peoples of the classical Orient. It was here, we learned at last, that writing was introduced toward the middle of the fourth millennium before Christianity. As early as 1905, Thureau-Dangin demonstrated that there had been a written language in the Near East other than Semitic and anterior to the Akkadian of which Babylonian and Assyrian represent only two dialects. Falkenstein, Jacobsen, Poebel, and Kramer, Sumerologists who deciphered and translated the first of the known scripts, are some of his successors.

As monosyllabic as Chinese or English; as rich in homophones, it would appear, as the Chinese, or very nearly; as unprovided with grammatical categories as classic Chinese, but enriched with determinatives which, according to circumstances, remind us of the role played

Youkaghir message on birchbark found in Siberia: "You are far away, you love a Russian woman who stands in my way; there will be children, you will have joy and a family. I will always think of you even if another man loves me."

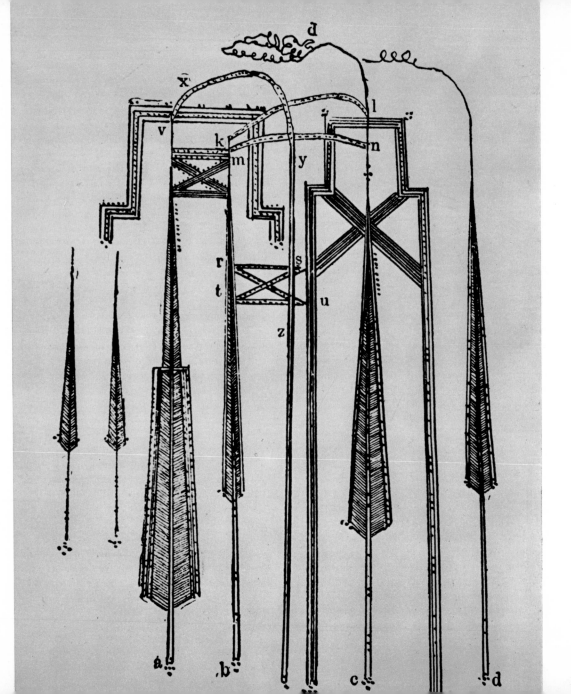

by the keys or the numerals in Chinese, 22
Sumerian is distinguished by its method of
writing in rebus-style. According to the con-
text, each of the Sumerian cuneiform signs
may either signify the name of the object
which it had reproduced originally or be
used only with its phonetic value. Consider,
for example, *she,* the grain, and *hu,* the bird.
Sometimes, the first signifies grain, the second,
bird. But, when combined phonetically, the
character *she* and the character *hu* convey the
idea of vision "without the slightest reference
either to a grain or a bird." (J. Bottéro.)
Transposing into the French language and
using the example proposed by Février, we
take the word *rapin* (art student). "Instead
of ... drawing, for instance, a man with a large
hat and a flowing artist's cravat, it is simpler
to juxtapose the drawing of a rat [pronounced
rah] and that of a pine [pronounced pa, as in
pat] which gives us *rapin.*"

When the evolution of cuneiforms is followed, from the first Sumerian ideograms to
the nearly three hundred signs which comprise
this script in its most highly stylized form, it
may be observed that it is composed at the
same time of ideograms, of determinatives
placed before or after the symbol of the word
which they are intended to qualify, of syllabic
signs indicating closed syllables (of the type
bar, kur, in French), of syllabic signs denot-
ing open syllables (of the type *ba, bi* or *ar, ir,*
again in French), and finally, of signs capable
of indicating diphthongs or isolated vowels.
Thus, Sumerian writing contains actually or

Rebus-writing of Dahomey.
Wooden door of the palace at Abomey.

potentially all the varieties of scripts deciphered as of today.

Am I wrong, then, to consider that Champollion had a greater mind than that of the god Thot himself, the supposed inventor of hieroglyphic writing? I am inclined to think, with Remy de Gourmont, that the invention of writing "seems to be a manifestation of intelligence rather than of genius," and that greater genius was required for Champollion to decipher the hieroglyphics than for the scribes to draw them.

To all this should be added that the decipherers enriched our literary, juridical, religious, and scientific knowledge no less than the circumnavigators of the sixteenth and seventeenth centuries. If George Smith, in 1861, had not read Tablet XI of the Babylonian epic of Gilgamesh, people would still be insisting that the Flood in the Bible belongs only to the Hebrew tradition. If Poebel, 53 years later, had not translated the Sumerian text which inspired both the Babylonian legend and its Hebraic adaptation, it might have been supposed that the Babylonians had invented a flood and a ship of righteous survivors. Moved as we are by the Lascaux cave paintings, the polychrome oxen of Jabbaren, or the antelopes of Tamrit in Tassili, we can only take pleasure in the pictures, which we do not understand since they lack inscriptions to make their meaning clear. The decipherers of scripts are thus the most precious auxiliaries of humanism. When a Sumerian tablet supplies us with a fragment of the code promulgated about 2050 B.C. by King Ur-Nammu and reveals to us a penal code which is infinitely more advanced than the Biblical law of retaliation, since the former only punished with fines both blows and injuries involving mutilation, then all our ideas about morality, or at least about the history of morality, are upset. Finally, it is the decipherers of writing

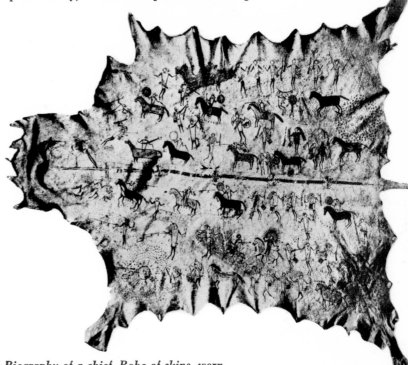

Biography of a chief. Robe of skins, worn by Sioux Indians of the Dakotas.

who help us to take stricter cognizance of the structure and of the specific characteristics of every script ever devised by man.

Actually, did man know how to read before he knew how to write? For me, there is no doubt that he did; on snow, on mud, on sand, man very soon identified the bird by the marks left by its steps; and he learned to distinguish the tracks of the tiger from those of the lion. The footprint of man in the mud was surely his first signature. Now, in the

Mayan hieroglyphs. Seventh century.

§ most ancient Chinese writings, it often happens that an offering is made to the footprint of an ancestor. And, furthermore, in the Chinese verb which signifies "recognize" or "discern" ⬚⬚ *pien*, it is indeed easy to discern the tracks of a savage beast, the brush strokes looking like the imprints of claws and the

points giving the impression of the fleshy parts. But where and when did writing begin? Some maintain that it was invented even before there was a spoken language. Father Tchang Tcheng-ming having declared a little hastily that a good many Chinese characters reproduce sign language, Father Van Ginnekennen inferred, even more hastily, that man wrote not only before he had a spoken language at his command, but even before he had worked out what the phoneticians call "clicks," those phonemes encountered in certain African or Caucasian languages. If it is true that more than one very ancient Chinese character expresses an abstract concept by means of the gesture which suggests it (friendship, by two joined hands), what is to be said except that all ideographic writing inevitably resorts to concrete images; so why should it not use a diagram of a gesture to express abstract ideas?

It remains to be decided where writing—in our present sense of the word—began. With the symbols of the Greek ambassadors, with the notches cut into the baker's stick, with the pre-Columbian quipus, with the strings knotted by the ancient Chinese? Or, did writing begin, as Voltaire has it, with "the painting of the voice," all the better, like a portrait, when there is a "good likeness"? Littré differentiates several kinds of writing: ideographic, "which directly represents ideas—for example, our punctuation marks"; syllabic, "which does not break down the syllables into vowels and consonants"; alphabetic, "which represents the sounds of the voice with the letters of an alphabet."

The quipus of Indian America did not really constitute writing any more than the knotted strings of the Far East did. Mnemonic devices for chronological purposes, inventories, accounts: that was their role. In the same way, we should not confuse with the characters of Chinese writing, the hexagrams of the *Yi King* or *Book of Changes,* themselves derived from the *Pa koua,* which the diviners composed with the help of finger-shaped rods in order to foresee the future. Let us rather compare these hexagrams with our packs of cards, with which the fortune teller pretends to foretell the future or reconstruct the past, according to the order in which the pictures turn up. Writing may truly be said to have begun only—and rudimentarily, at that—with pictography. Still, one might claim that the picture which we call figurative or representational is a pictogram. Actually, the transition is almost imperceptible between what is properly called representational painting and what is properly called the pictogram. Those stations of the cross in our churches which told the illiterate about the halting places and the sufferings of Calvary—do they differ so much from the pictograms with which the Eskimo tells about the course of a hunt and his mishaps? Do not innumerable stylizations of the human body in prehistoric paintings imperceptibly though inevitably lead to the ideograms which represent a man or a woman? Of course, it is a far cry from the "accounts of winter," with which the Dakota Indians symbolized the end of the year, to the Chinese chronicles of *Springs and Autumns.* In the

Chichimec story. Mexican manuscript.
Paper made of agave plant.
Fifteenth century.

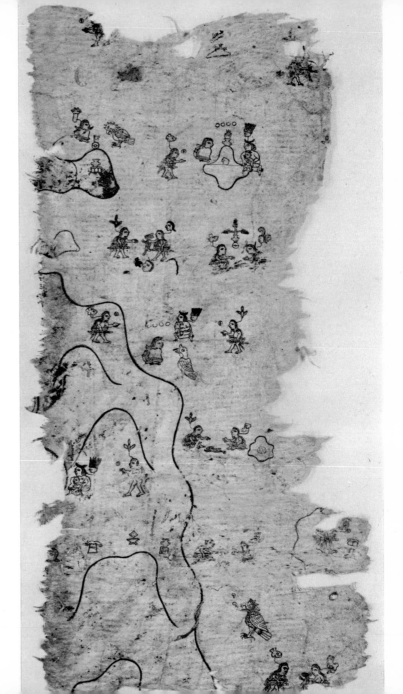

first case, we are still very close to the picto-grams of the Eskimos; but in the second case, we are undoubtedly in the midst of "word" writing.

Besides the notches and the knots, besides the scripts which Février calls synthetic and Cohen calls proto-writings, recent historians readily distinguish systems in which the signs in one stroke suggest a phrase and other systems which, by breaking down the verbal flow, indicate isolated words; and those systems, finally, which, by analyzing each of the words, make evident the vowel and consonant sounds (these are phonetic writings, sometimes syllabic, sometimes alphabetical).

The three most important "word" scripts are the Sumerian, the Egyptian, and the Chinese, the first now considered to be the source of the other two.

Even if the etymologies of the *Chouo wen* and those of Father Tchang Tcheng-ming are disputed, it cannot be denied that Chinese writing, like Sumerian, is based on drawings representing either concrete objects or symbols. Chinese philologists distinguish between the images or representations (*wen*) and the combined characters (*tseu*). The images are separated from the rest as representations (*siang-hing*), 364 of them in the *Chouo wen*, and as symbols, which some prefer to call dactylograms (*tche che*), of which the *Chouo wen* records 125. The combined characters are themselves subdivided into logical aggregates and into phonetic or phonic complexes. The logical aggregates (*houei-yi*) are composed of two or more simpler characters brought to-

Tracing of an annotated Tibetan manuscript.

gether by the sequence of ideas which is being suggested. Take the character *ling* 靈. We recognize in it: (a) the rain 雨, (b) three mouths 口口口; (c) the character which sig-

Cast of a seal from Mohenjo-Daro with characters. Third millennium B.C.

nifies sorcerer 巫. This is itself explained by a logical aggregate: two men 人人 who are using a square 工 (whence the idea of geo-mancy, of sorcery). All is now clear: the men

provided with a square, in other words, the magicians, are making incantations — three mouths—so that it will rain. From this, we deduce the idea of supernatural power. That is why, in the Chinese of the Jesuits, the word *ling* 靈 at last came to signify the *soul* of the Catholic theologians.

As for the phonetic or phonic complexes, those which Février calls morpho-phonograms, only one of the elements of the character conveys the sense; the other indicates the sound, though often not precisely. Take the character *chan* or *san* 彡. Standing alone, it means, by virtue of *wen*, that is, as an image, hair of the beard, hair of the head, or line. In the complex character *su* 須, which means beard, the element *chan* or *san* combined with the character signifying head 頁, forms a logical aggregate designating the hair which covers the lower part of the face. In turn, the characters *san* (the Japan cedar, *Cryptomeria* 杉) and *chan* (drizzling rain 参), the element *san* may at the same time be interpreted in its capacity of logical aggregate (a tree, the leaves of which are as fine as hair; and rain, itself as fine as hair) and as a guide for the pronunciation of the character. Very often, in the logical aggregates, one of the elements serves as a key, as in the character *su*, beard.

Chinese philologists have isolated two other categories of characters: the *tchouan-tchou* and the *kia-tseu*. The first expression refers to words of derivative meaning, the second, to faulty borrowed words, of which certain ones exhibit a simple copying error traditionally transmitted out of respect, but most of which were deliberately chosen. Thus, the character which signifies ten thousand is written *wan*

萬, which depicts a scorpion, stylized but still quite recognizable. The Chinese had several signs for this animal, one of which was pronounced *wan*. Since there was no character to denote the number ten thousand, which was also pronounced *wan*, they indicated ten thousand, pronounced *wan*, by using that character (from among the many scorpion signs) which was pronounced in the same way.

In a system of this kind, how can words be classified? The Chinese were undecided. Their oldest dictionary, the *Eul Ya*, divided everything into sixteen categories: heaven, earth, man, mountain, water, and so on. The authors of the *Chouo wen* divided the characters according to 540 keys, each of which suggests a different idea; but as certain of these keys accounted for many characters and certain of them for very few, the lexicographers later eliminated the more deficient series and arbitrarily divided the characters among those keys which were the best supplied. The Chinese were interested in graphic resemblances, not at all, alas, in logic. Under the Ming dynasty, the keys were reduced to 214, and the list was stabilized in the celebrated dictionary of K'ang Hi, emperor of the Ts'ing dynasty (1653-1722). Until the reform of 1956 which reduced the number of keys to 187, the system remained in force, but concurrently with others, particularly one which governs the dictionaries called *yun-fou* and the most famous of which is known as the *P'ei-wen yun-fou*; the ideograms in this system are classified phonetically, according to the method

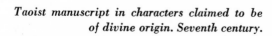

Taoist manuscript in characters claimed to be of divine origin. Seventh century.

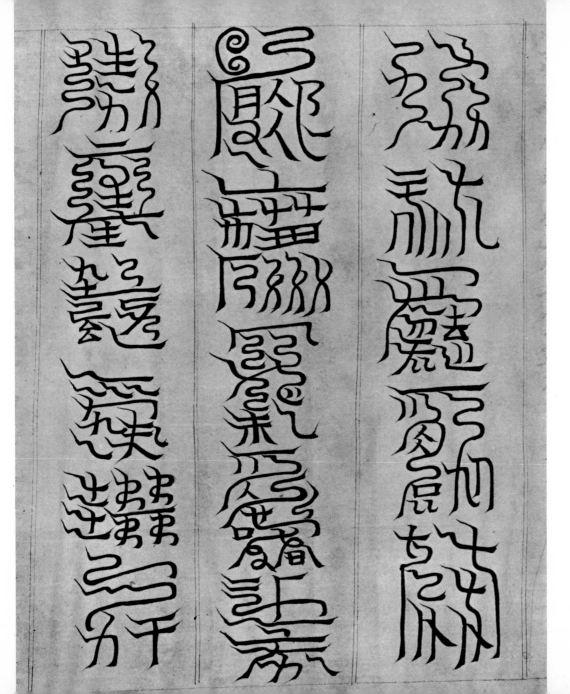

訓於後昆此人無為大聖碣其力我尊也然昔之池谷澗宮城之

of the *fan ts'ie* which, to determine the pronunciation of a character, furnishes two characters, the first of which supplies the initial consonant and the second, the end of the word. A character which is to be pronounced *louo* will thus be followed by one character which is pronounced *li* and by another which is pronounced *mouo*; for example: *l + ouo = louo.*

Through the prestige of Chinese Buddhism, this script, perfectly adapted to a monosyllabic language and lacking in inflections, spread to Japan, a country with a polysyllabic language rich in particles, or affixes. The Japanese were thus led to use, on the one hand, ideograms having their own phonetic value, and, on the other hand, ideograms conserving the meaning they had in Chinese, but sometimes with a pronunciation almost like that of the Chinese, sometimes with the pronunciation of the Japanese word signifying the same thing. Thus, the Chinese character which signifies mountain and is pronounced *chan* is used in Japanese in the same sense, but it is pronounced *yama*, as in Fuji-Yama. In the same way, the following three characters 山本山 which in Chinese would be pronounced *chan, pen, chan*, in Japanese become the proper noun *Yamamotoyama.* Inevitably, what happened to the Akkadian ideograms borrowed from a writing system intended to notate Sumerian, recurred in Japan and led to polyphony; the Chinese character *jen* (人) is sometimes pronounced *gin* in Japanese, sometimes *nin*, and, when it denotes what it means in Chinese and Japanese, that is, a man, it is pronounced *hito.*

It is easy to understand that the Japanese

Chinese stamping (print making).

soon sought to write their language in the most convenient way for them. Starting from a Chinese cursive, they went on to devise a system of phonetic notations, the *kana. Hirakana* and *kata-kana* are merely two graphic variants with similar syllabic separation (48 signs in each system). One might suppose that by now the Japanese would have discarded the imported ideograms and written their language entirely in phonetic signs, in *kana.* Not at all. In spite of the development of a society which favored only the *kana* and despite the directives formulated by the Ministry of National Education, which ordained a sparing use of Chinese characters, these not only stood their ground in literature and the press, but even multiplied in the scientific vocabulary where they play a role something like that of the Greek roots with us. These Chinese characters have in no way impeded the progress of Japanese science, no matter what the enemies of ideograms may have written on the subject.

Besides the Sumerian and the Chinese, the other great ancient script, and one which is partly a script with words, is the Egyptian. Very different from the Sumerian and the Chinese, the Egyptian, close in this respect to the Semitic languages, is firmly based on a system of consonantal roots wherein the vocal play or shading makes the meaning clear. But, unlike Chinese writing, Egyptian, as is evident in the earliest texts at our disposal, is comprised of signs, certain of which are pure ideograms, while others have phonetic value, and still others have to be read like Sumerian rebuses. There are definite features of Sumerian writing here and the evidence, perhaps, of borrowing, an influence all the more probable

because the hieroglyphics seem to have originated in the delta region and not in Upper Egypt.

Why didn't the Egyptians elaborate a coherent system based on this principle which they had discovered: a notation not only phonetic, like the *kana*, but actually consonantal, considering the fact that the Egyptian script had been able to isolate 24 consonantal signs capable of notating all the Egyptian words? It would be foolish to accuse the Egyptians of not having understood their invention, or suspect the Japanese of not having been aware that their *kanas* indicate sounds. Let us rather accept as true the fact that, jealous as we know civilizations to have been of their languages, they were much less concerned about their scripts. Seduced or conquered, the one by Chinese writing, the other by Sumerian, the Japanese and Egyptian civilizations openly conserved the survivals which appear to us deviations from the graphic system of the language which was their model.

Ignoring the Maya and Aztec scripts, about which we have been condemned by Spanish barbarism to know too little, and certainly will be so condemned for a long time to come, of all the "word" scripts, only the Chinese remained strictly true to its principle, the Sumerian and the Egyptian each having proceeded toward syllabic or consonantal notation.

None of these three great "word" scripts finally became an alphabetical writing system. Of course, it was maintained for a long time that the alphabet of the Phoenicians was directly inspired by Egyptian writing, but scholars have repudiated this hypothesis. Successive attempts were made to relate the Phoenician alphabet to Akkadian or Cypriote syllabaries, to proto-Sinaitic writing, even to that of the Philistines—those "Nordics"—because certain "savants" could not tolerate the idea that Semites, people of a "race" presumed inferior, had given the alphabet to man. Today, there is no hesitation in recognizing the originality of the Phoenician merchants.

The Near East elaborated at least three writing systems of an alphabetical type: the Ugaritic, the Sinaitic, and the Phoenician, all three of which have consonants. Dhorme and Bauer in 1919 deciphered the Ugaritic alphabet of Ras Shamra, or, at least, one of the alphabets of Ras Shamra, the one which is comprised of 30 signs and which, similar in appearance to cuneiform characters, is almost completely consonantal. A very recent communication from Charles Virolleaud to the Académie des Inscriptions et Belles-Lettres proves that besides the cuneiform alphabet of 30 signs, known since 1929, Ras Shamra used another alphabet of 22 signs, written from right to left, and not from left to right. The closeness of this Ugaritic alphabet of 22 signs to the Phoenician alphabet of 22 signs is much too evident to be considered a mere accident.

Thus, thanks to the different systems of writing, as we get to know more about the past history of man in the Near East, the points of agreement become more numerous and more evident than the points of difference. In any case, perfected by the Phoenicians for their commercial needs, as we believe, this consonantal alphabet was to fructify not only the Semitic world through the media of the Aramaic, Estrangelo, Syriac, Hebrew, and

Chinese calligraphy.

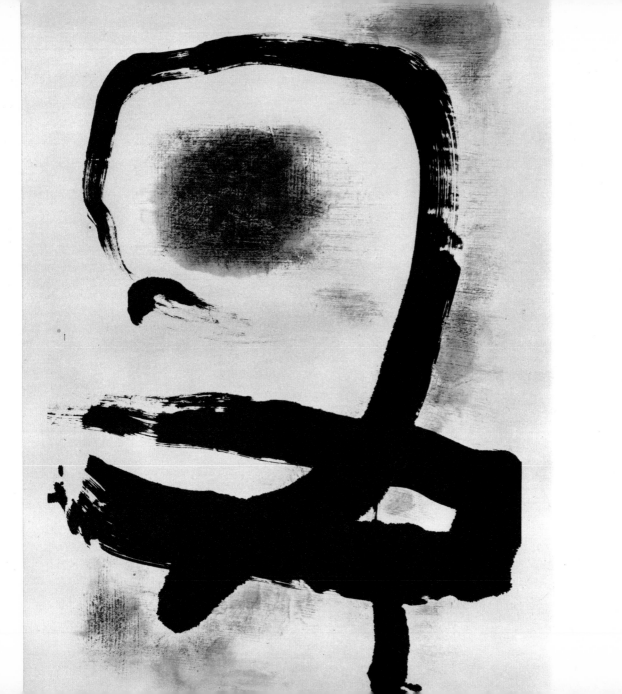

Arabic alphabets. And this was to happen in spite of the serious inconvenience of a system which could only indicate consonants clearly, since neither the *matres lectionis,* those consonants used in Punic, Moabite, or paleo-Hebraic scripts to help the reader (but how vaguely!) to pronounce the vowels, nor the vowel points of the Hebrew, nor the vocalic signs of Arabic completely solve the problem of vowel notation.

Consider the triliteral Arabic root, K T B. Vocally, this could be *katib* كَاتِب the writer; *kitab* كِتَاب the book; *kataba* كَتَبَ he wrote; *kutub* كُتُب the books. Or consider the root W Z N وزن, *wazana* وَزَنَ he weighs; *wuzina* وُزِنَ he has been weighed. But in newspaper writing, for example, the vowels are not indicated, and it is the construction of the sentence which informs the reader about the vocalism that must be added to the consonantal skeleton, كتب or وزن. Since the Phoenician alphabet is the source of ours and of the word *alphabet* itself, it might be well to explain briefly the names of the signs in this script. The first letter of the Phoenician alphabet is pronounced *alf.* Now, *alf* signifies an ox. The archaic way of writing *alf* actually does suggest the head of an ox. The second consonant is pronounced *bet;* this is also the Phoenician name for house. Now, the design of this consonant suggests either the Egyptian hieroglyphic which means house ⊓, or the sign which, in the proto-sinaitic

"The Emperor Hiuen Tsong summons his town officials from time to time and obliges them to compose their calligraphy in his presence, so that he may be assured of their abilities." Chinese silk painting of the eighteenth century.

inscriptions, indicates the consonant B ⊓. The letters of the Phoenician alphabet, at least the first ones, those from which we get the word *alphabet,* were thus given names by what is

Chinese sigillary (seal) characters by Tchao Mong-fou.

called the acrophonic method. Although the acrophonic interpretation does not perfectly account for all the letters of the Phoenician alphabet, it is hard not to be moved, as members of our own civilization, by this obscure and slow process whereby, for instance, the Phoenician consonant *res* (the name of which, by acrophony, is deduced from the word, head —and the shape actually does suggest a profile) ends up as the Greek *rho* (ρ) in which one would have to be most ingenious to recognize still the most abstract outline of a man's face.

In spite, then, of the very evident imperfection, from our viewpoint, of a strictly consonantal script, the more evident, in fact, since our Indo-European languages are not constructed, like the Semitic languages, on a consonantal skeleton, the Phoenician and Arabic scripts have known—and are, indeed, still pursuing—a prodigious career. After all, the order in which Phoenician consonants are recited was transmitted to the Etruscans; and we find Arabic script, concentrated, rapid in its outline, harmonious in its forms, and powerfully aided by the spread of Islam, gaining a little ground everywhere in the world: it is even used to transcribe languages of very different structures like Turkish, Iranian, and Swahili. The obvious advantage offered man by the Semitic alphabet was made manifest even in Sogdiana, which it reached through the activities of the caravan merchants. In recent times, in Uzbekistan, and in spite of Soviet law, Arabic script has returned to prominence, reappearing on Mohammedan calendars and serving the Uzbeks as stenographic notation, in preference to the Cyrillic script. As for the Ethiopian syllabary, which ingeniously modifies the way of writing each consonant in order to indicate the adjacent vowel, it is clear that this alphabet was capable of advancing toward what we call the alphabet,

that is, a system which is able to indicate vowels as well as consonants. It remains to be determined whether the Ethiopians took from the Indian syllabaries this idea of writing the vowels or whether it is more proper to note an influence here of the Greek script, conveyed by Christianity which, in turn, is transmitted by the Greek script.

Ingeniously adapted as they were to Semitic languages, the alphabets of the Phoenician type could not adequately indicate an Indo-European language, like Greek. And syllabic notation was hardly appropriate either, as is evident when the Cypriote syllabary or the Creto-Mycenean Linear B is studied. Indeed, compare the Cypriote *pa-si-le-u-se* with the Greek *basileus* (βασιλεύς). Since the Semitic consonants do not correspond to those of the Greek and, moreover, as the Greek language cannot do without written vowels, and, as it seems, anyway, that the human mind only asks itself questions which it can answer (even when trying to prove that there is no answer), we must suppose that the difficulties of the Semitic alphabet, by challenging the Greek scribes, encouraged and helped them to find an answer. The fact, also, that the Cretan, like the Cypriote, syllabary uses at the same time syllabic signs, vocalic signs, and, in certain circumstances, signs of consonantal value when the vowel is, so to speak, spirited away or suppressed, could have stimulated the Greeks to combine vocalic and consonantal signs in two complementary systems, the blending of which finally formed what we call the alphabet. Although they retained the order and the

Print by Utamaro.

Japanese calligraphy on cloth.

vowels, *alpha, epsilon, omicron, upsilon,* four of the consonants which were transmitted to them, *iota* being an innovation. Toward the fourth century B.C., the experimentation period was over and the different Greek alphabets united at the same time as a common language was developed from the diverse Hellenic dialects. From then on, the Greek alphabet, which had proved itself, was to continue its progress: the Greek alphabet of Bishop Wulfila owes it much, as does the Coptic alphabet, which borrowed 24 of its letters, the 7 others deriving from the ultimate form of Egyptian script, the demotic.

Some scholars believe that the Armenian alphabet, so perfectly adapted to its language, with its thirty-one consonants and its five vowels, is only an arrangement of the alphabet of the Hellenes. It seems, in any case, that the Georgian script is related to the Greek alphabet, and it is certain that the ancient alphabet of the Etruscans was inspired by the alphabets of Western Greece. Thanks to the spread of the Orthodox religion, and later, because of the gains of communism, the Cyrillic alphabet perpetuated the Greek script after having incorporated into it Glagolitic characters.

As for knowing where, when, and how the alphabet we call Latin was constituted, an alphabet which appears particularly important to us because it is our own, it is still too soon to decide these matters. This newcomer remains a mystery to us. That it derives from a Greek alphabet of a Western type seems to be an accepted fact today, but was it borrowed directly from the Greeks of Chalcis? And what does it owe to the Etruscans? Before the unification, under the Roman Empire, of what we call Italy, since the Western Greek alpha-

names of the Semitic letters: *alpha, beta, gamma,* and so on, the Greeks thought of using, to indicate the sounds which were peculiar to them, the letters signifying those Semitic consonants which their own language lacked, and to use for the indication of their

bets produced all sorts of local alphabets—Messapian, Sicel, Oscan, Faliscan, Umbrian, Picenian, etc.—it is best to be cautious. All we know for the moment is that the farflung Roman conquests disseminated the twenty-three letters of the Latin alphabet, to which the medieval Christians added the definitive distinction between the *i* and the *j,* and between the *u* and the *v.*

In contradiction of those self-styled scholars who could not tolerate the idea that the alphabet was an invention of the Semites, James Février stated publicly that "the Aryan spirit felt something of an aversion to writing; perhaps there was something here of an old tendency common to the Indo-European world," a point which the Druidic tradition would bear out. When the Aryans settled in the valley of the Indus, on the site of Mohenjo-daro, where the prevailing culture already included a knowledge of writing, they brought with them only an oral literature. Février continues: "Even the word for book, *pustaka,* is not found in the old texts and seems to have come from the Iranian *post* (skin). Besides, it must have been diverted very early from its etymological meaning because, from the Indian viewpoint, it is an abomination to write on skin." Whatever discomfort it may have cost our Nazis, the history of writing confirms the fact that Brahmi and Kharoshthi, the two graphic systems used in India at the time of the celebrated Emperor Asoka (273?-232? B.C.), are of Semitic origin. Kharoshthi, especially, which is written from right to left, shows, even in the form of its characters, the

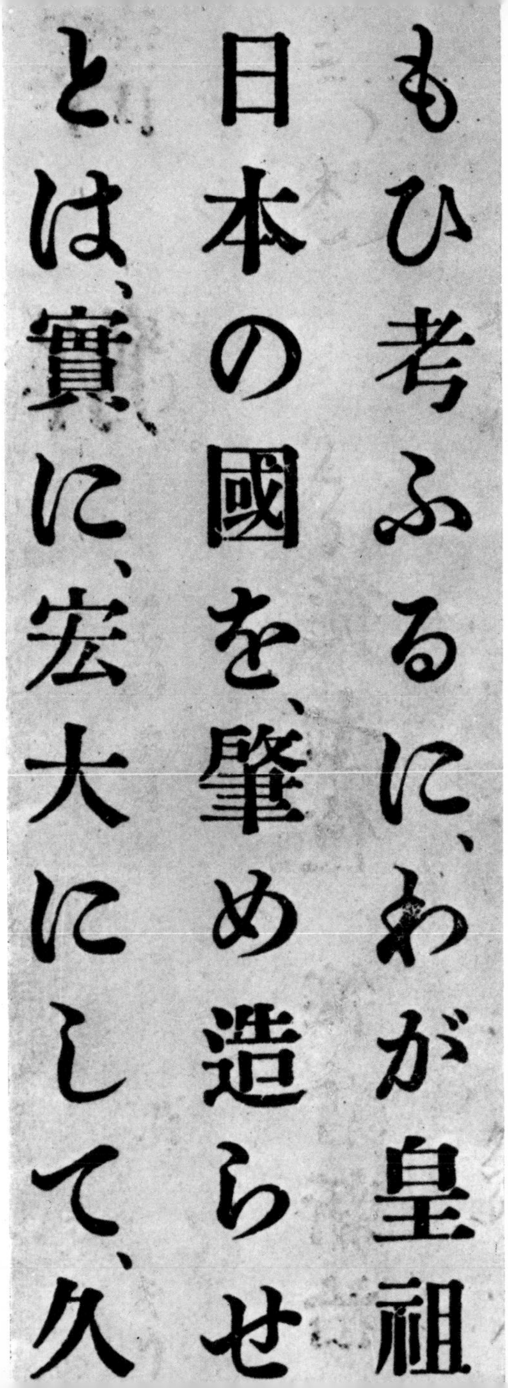

Japanese characters.

もひ考ふるに、わが皇祖
日本の國を、肇め造らせ
とは、實に、宏大にして、久

8

traces of its Semitic affiliation. Brahmi, which is somewhat more removed from it, has had a more vigorous existence than Kharoshthi: from India to Central Asia and the Far East, many scripts were influenced by it, scripts more or less well adapted to the languages they had to notate, many not even of an Indo-European type.

The most functional is incontestably the Devanagari, word for word; the so-called "writing of the gods," this form of Brahmi first notated ancient Sanskrit, the sacred language whose privileges the Brahmins at the beginning bestowed upon themselves. Then, this script notated Hindi, the great Indo-European language which is spoken in India today. "Its most noticeable characteristic is the long horizontal bar, the 'potence' ('gallows'), called *matra,* which follows the line almost without interruption, uniting not only the syllables but often the words, and below which are attached the characters, except for some vowel signs which are inscribed above." (Février.) Although Tamil and Telugu belong to the group of Dravidian languages, and Tibetan, which is closely related to Chinese, belongs to the group sometimes called Sino-Tibetan, sometimes Tibeto-Burman, these languages have adapted, more or less adequately, the Brahmi syllabary. This proves to us once again that the peoples of the world cherish their spoken languages more than their scripts.

Any history of writing to be even adequately detailed should be at least one thousand pages long. So it is clear that I can only suggest here a few of the principal solutions devised by men in six thousand years to capture the most divergent languages in their writing systems. I wish I could convey an inkling of the truth which Meillet understood when he declared that the men who invented and perfected writing were "prodigious linguists." And, if we admit with Cournot that the "critical epoch" in the history of the human mind dates from the invention of writing, then man's woefully brief spiritual history was, perhaps, not entirely useless.

Gourmont was right when he states: "The thousands of little conveniences, the petty modern luxuries conceal the essential point of civilization from us. By being deprived of them, we often learn to appreciate their uselessness; but there is one very stable, very ancient element of which man cannot be deprived without ceasing to be a human being. Now, we have only to think about it to realize that this ancient element is not only the most useful, but the most beautiful as well. Without printing, the Celto-Germanic civilization might have been possible; without writing, however, no intellectual civilization is conceivable. Writing, then, surpasses printing in significance, and the moment in human history which gave it birth is thus a greater and more beautiful moment. The unknowns (it was not Gutenberg) who invented printing in the fifteenth century..." Enough of that! Gourmont was right up to this point (Gutenberg actually did not invent printing), but he was wrong to state that it was perfected in the fifteenth century by "unknowns." No, they were not as "unknown" as all that.

Tradition credits the eunuch Ts'ai Louen with the honor of having announced to the

Inscription from the Koran in quadrangular Kufic script.

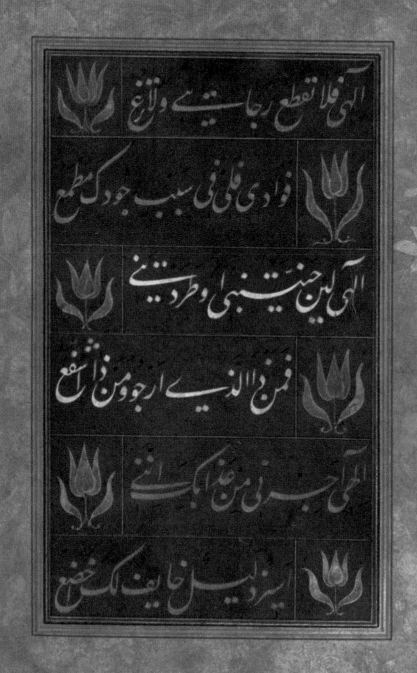

الهٰی فلا تقطع رجاء نتے ولا تَقطع

فؤادی فلبی فی سبیب جودک مطمع

الهٰی لین حنیت نینی و طردتینی

فمن ذا الذی ارجو و من ذا اشفع

الهٰی اجبرنی من عندک باننی

یا یزن لیل خایف لک خضع

emperor of China, in 105 A.D., the invention of a new material, paper. When Sir Aurel Stein had a scrap of paper analyzed in Europe, a shred he had excavated from a spur of the Great Wall, and which he attributed to about the year 150, it was revealed to the West that the Chinese not only had known for a very long time how to make paper with vegetable fibers, but they knew about what we call pure rag paper. From then on, paper traveled slowly toward the West. In the third century, the new product arrived in Turkestan. The oldest manuscripts found by Pelliot on the site of Touen-houang date back to the first years of the fifth century. In 1957, as I was examining, near the "Caves of the Thousand Buddhas," the paper which the artisans of the oasis used to make there out of the leaves of the ma-lan, the desert iris, I learned from Jacques Gernet that the paper has exactly the same texture, the same markings, the same quality as that of the manuscripts of Touen-houang which are to be found in the French national library. As far back as the fifth century, paper replaced silk and bamboo in Turkestan as a writing material. About this time, too, a black ink, very similar to the kind we call India ink, became known; a little later, it occurred to someone to coat with red cinnabar those seals which played such a great role in Chinese tradition. The seal, ink or cinnabar, paper—all the elements necessary for the art of printing—were at hand. So obvious to the Chinese is the relationship between the seal and printing that the same character yin 印 still means to-

Model of Arabic calligraphy.
Nineteenth century.

day, on the one hand, the seal that the Han emperors knew and, on the other, printing, in the present sense of the word. Pressed into argil, a soft clay, and intended to authenticate

Calligraphy: an Arabic prayer. St. Sofia.

documents, the seal of the Han dynasty was certainly not movable type. Nevertheless, as soon as this signature in sigillary characters was covered with ink and stamped on a piece of paper, printing began. What slow, tortuous progress before the first Taoist seals, used

Pages 44/45: Arab "calligram"
of the nineteenth century.

قلا...
وسع...

إنَّ الَّذِينَ آمَنُوا وَعَمِلُوا الصَّ...
لهم

especially with an eye to magic practices, the first imprints from the Confucian classics incised in stone, or the first woodblocks engraved by the Buddhist monks were to become

Model of Persian script. Nineteenth century.

our rotary presses which print eight million copies daily of the *Asahi*, the *London Times*, the *New York Times*, or *France-Soir!* Let us try to retrace this path.

The *Heou Han Chou*, the annals of the late Han dynasty, informs us that, as early as 175

A.D., the Confucian classics were carved on stone so that the vital texts might be preserved. Obviously, it was not possible to make imprints of them before the invention of paper and ink. The earliest stamped inscriptions which have come down to us date from the first half of the seventh century, which is hardly surprising since ink was not known until the fifth. This does not mean that the technique was not practiced before that time.

Introduced in Samarkand about 650 A.D., paper was produced there about one century later. About 700, it appeared in Mecca; about 800, in the valley of the Nile; that is, very soon after the setting up in Baghdad of the first paper mills. About the middle of the ninth century, it arrived in Spain, where it was produced in 1150. It was only then that it penetrated into Italy. Three-quarters of a century later, it came to Germany. At the beginning of the fourteenth century, it crossed the Channel and reached England, but it was not produced there until about two centuries later; whereas France, since 1189, Italy, since 1276, and Germany, since 1391, already had their own paper-making mills. For more than five centuries, the Chinese had been the only ones in the world who knew how to fabricate the new material; certain prisoners in Samarkand had revealed the secret to the Arabs who then jealously guarded it for five more centuries before teaching it to the Spaniards. However, there was still no question of printing in the West.

But, as early as 770, magico-religious formulas in Sanskrit and in Chinese characters

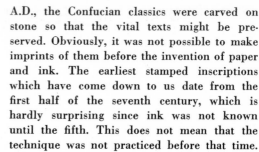

Monogram of the Sultan Ibrahim I. 1647.

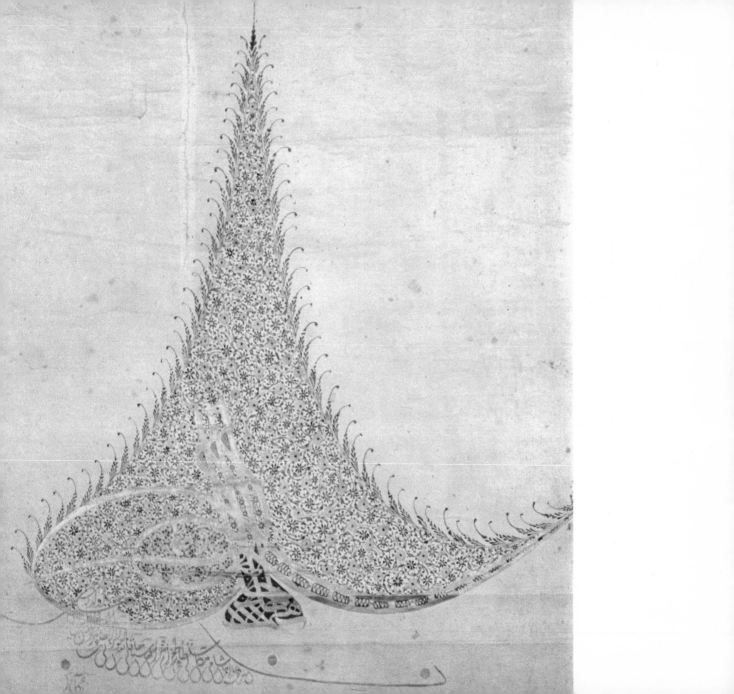

were printed on wood in Japan. Out of devotion to Buddhism, the Empress Shokotu ordered a million charms to be block-printed on paper from wooden matrices and distributed in a million miniature pagodas. Carter perspicaciously recognized here one of the great milestones in the history of our planet. Under the T'ang dynasty (618-907), there was much printing in China, especially in Szechuan, of school handbooks and books about magic. Not much is known about this ancient period of printing, but thanks to Paul Pelliot, who discovered in Touen-houang a copy of the *Diamond Sutra,* we are able to read in it that: "this book was printed by Wang Kie on May 11, 868, and is to be distributed free to all, to perpetuate with profound respect the memory of his parents." Here he is, then—and not Gutenberg—the earliest printer whose name is known to us.

Although the magic formulas of the Taoists encouraged the reproduction of some charms, it is to Buddhism principally and to the rival doctrine, Confucianism, that we owe the progress of the technique which we call printing. Paradoxically, and yet naturally enough, how could any ideology, any religion, deny itself the opportunity of benefiting from facilities which put at its disposal an endless reproduction of its formularies, its sacred texts, and its commandments? The paradox, of course, is that superstition, faith, and dogmatism did much to stimulate the progress of the technique which was to encourage, at least for some time, knowledge and criticism of religions. Now, there's an unforeseen effect of "dialectics"!

Spanish Haggadah. Fourteenth century.

Actually, the Chinese used printing concurrently to diffuse, on the one hand, the religious texts of Buddhism and, on the other, the canonical texts of a philosophy opposed to the propagation of the sutras: Confucianism. During atrocious civil wars and while four dynasties of the five which gave their names to this period succeeded one another, China brought out the first great classic edition of the Confucianist canon. And this was a time about as horrible in China (907-960) as that which was transpiring then in the West during the death agony of the last Carolingians (at the moment when our culture was at its lowest level; and I recall in what terms, a short time before his death, Focillon described this period for me, a period to him one of the blackest the West has known). China, ravaged by at least as harrowing a civil war and as intense feudal dissension as were soon to engulf France, nevertheless produced this great literary work. Except for a Japanese edition of the *Eul-ya,* however, in which the characters, according to the colophon, had been engraved by the calligrapher who worked for Fong Tao, nothing has come down to us of this prodigious work. But what we can glimpse of the Chinese classics through this great man encourages us to think that as early as the tenth century this minister was as powerful an influence on the art of printing, notably the printing of the Sung dynasty (960-1279), as the Gutenberg Bible was on Western typography.

Not long after the Confucianist classics, an extensive Buddhist canon was printed in China, about 972; and in about the year 1000, the great dynastic histories. It was then that printing knew its golden age in China, its

time of glory and of greatest technical perfection. Collectors have transmitted to us some original editions, about a thousand years old, the quality of which, in the judgment of con-

*Marie of France at her writing desk.
Thirteenth century miniature.*

g noisseurs, has never been equaled. Even though many Arabs lived in the China of the T'ang and that of the Sung empire, their religious prejudices deterred them from transmitting this diabolical invention to the West: in order

to ink the paper, had not the Chinese shamelessly used brushes fabricated with bristles from pigs?

In order for printing to reach us, it needed the waves of Mongol invasions, the ebbing which followed, and the many deputations or missions dispatched to the Khans by Saint Louis and the papacy. Departing from Lyon on April 16, 1245, Jean du Plan Carpin reached Karakorum on July 22, 1246, just in time to be present at the enthroning of the new Khan, Guyuk. He returned to Rome in 1247, bearer of a message which invited the princes of the Occident to submit themselves to the Mongols. The envoy of Saint Louis, Rubrouk, received hardly more encouragement from the Khan, Mongka, whom he met seven years later. Just the same, these two political rebuffs permitted Europe to learn a little about those who were called at that time the Cathaians, the people of Cathay, our Chinese. Many other missionaries left for China at about this time: in 1247, several Dominicans; about 1250, André de Longjumeau and Jean de Carcassonne; in 1289, Jean de Monte Corvino, who became the first bishop of Khanbalik, or Cambaluc, at the site of what we call Peiping. Christians and Mongols were then united by hatred of a common enemy, Islam; this was proved by attempts at alliance between Saint Louis and Mongka and by the famous *Faits des Tartares,* the exploits of the Tartars, which Clovis Brunel attributes to the Dominican David d'Ashby, who lived for ten years among the Mongols

*Saint Ambrose: Hexameron.
Illuminated letters
of the Corbie school. Eighth century.*

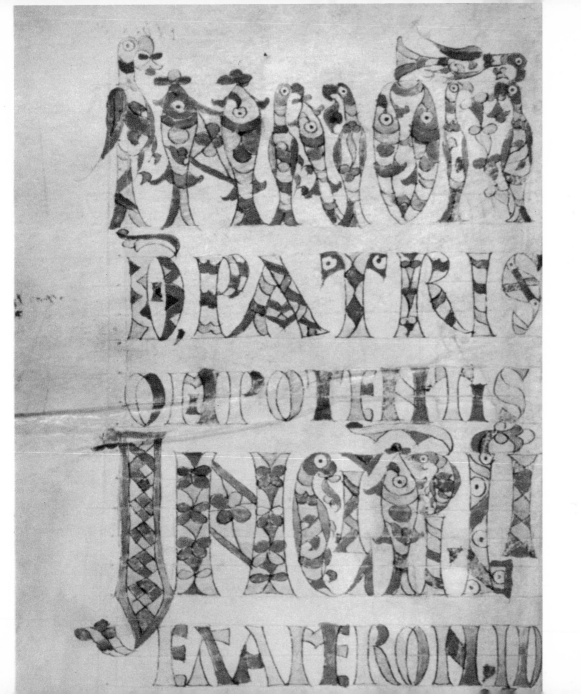

ANNON
D PATRIS
OMPOTENTIS
INCPL
EXAFERONID

and then, at the time of the Council of Lyon in 1274, presented the ambassadors of the Great Khan to Pope Gregory X.

These Mongols, whom legend has painted for us as savage brutes, practiced a political and religious tolerance unknown in Christendom and diffused through printing the works of the Chinese civilization which they had subdued by arms. Besides almanacs, we also possess, thanks to them, a series of engravings intended for the general public and entitled: "Beautiful women who, from dynasty to dynasty, have made empires crumble." From which, it may be remarked that these so-called barbarians were no more so than those persons among us who make a comfortable living, indeed, by divulging in print the alleged amours of Edward VIII and Mrs. Simpson, of Margaret and Townsend, of Soraya and her Shah, of Marilyn Monroe and her various husbands. From the very start, apparently, printing had found its path: religious feeling and sex. I am not forgetting that it also produced playing cards and paper money, which at least eight travelers of that period described for us, Marco Polo in these terms:

"All these sheets of paper bear the seal of His Majesty, without which they are worthless. They are fabricated with as much form and ceremony as if they were made of pure gold or silver, for a number of specially appointed officers subscribe their names on each note, each one affixing his seal. And when this has been properly done, their principal officer, appointed by His Majesty, having dipped the royal seal committed to his custody

Illuminated letter with portrait of Charles V.

into cinnabar, stamps the piece of paper with it, and the form of the seal tinged with the vermilion remains impressed upon it. After that, it becomes usable money. And the act

Fragment of Burgundy banner.
Fifteenth century.

of counterfeiting it is punished as a capital offense unto the third generation. Different marks are imprinted according to the intended purpose of the note. His Majesty made such tremendous quantities of these sheets of paper that he would be able to buy all the treasures of the world with them, and it would not cost him anything!"

5

Diploma of Charlemagne. December 6, 777.

Not long afterwards, at the beginning of the fourteenth century, Rachid Ed-Din described in detail, in Persian and Arabic, the Chinese technique of printing as it was practiced before the invention of movable characters. It was at this time that the first engravings were being printed in Europe. A short time before, letters inscribed in Chinese sigillary characters had reached the kings of France. It was at about this time also that paper money written in Arabic and Chinese began to be printed in Tabriz under Mongol influence, and this despite the terrible financial crisis following the inflationary period which had cruelly affected China in the twelfth century, some decades after the socialistic experiment of Wang Ngan-che.

Thus, it was due to the Mongols that the Chinese invention was spread to the Christian West. But already, in his *Treatise on Agriculture,* the Chinese Wang Tcheng had revealed the technique of movable wooden characters. It was as if Europe was always to lag behind! When the first printed texts were being engraved there on wood, Korea had already instituted movable metal characters and pro-

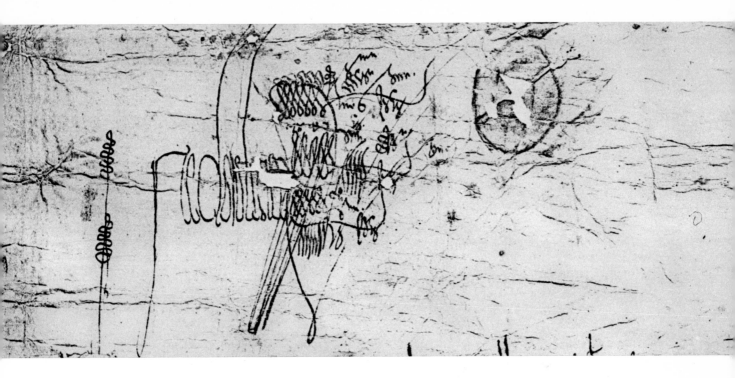

duced books using this process. The second font of Korean characters dates from 1420, the third from 1434. Is it then mere chance that the first European printers settled in Venice, Prague, and in the Bavarian towns? In the course of their campaigns, the Mongol armies had reached these regions, and the Turks, as we already know, did not hold printing in low esteem. Among the documents excavated in the region of Turfan by the Prussian Expedition, the most numerous texts are printed in Chinese, in Sanskrit, and *in Ugrian*. To any unprejudiced mind, history, there-fore, is perfectly clear: the invention of paper, the invention of ink, stamping, books engraved on wood, movable wooden characters, even movable metal characters—all of these were invented in China, improved in Korea, and known for a long time in Japan. It was in China and in Chinese Turkestan, long before Gutenberg's Bible, that books were printed, secular as well as sacred.

Having admitted this, we can go on to say that, in the same way that the Europeans knew how to extract those benefits from gun-powder and the compass which the Chinese had neglected or disdained, so it happened that the scope and dissemination of printing in the West were such as to culminate in the great daily newspapers and the five billion books which our publishers pour out yearly upon our planet. But, even the daily press or the weekly press is not an invention of the West. Our countries had not as yet the slightest idea of the existence of printing when the Chinese were running a gazette, the *K'ai-yuan tsa-pao*, published in the seventh century for the T'ang, specimens of which have come down to us. Let us observe at this point that already the word *pao* 報 was being used, the same word which we recognize in 1960 in the title of the large Communist daily of Peking (Peiping), the *Jen-min je pao*.

That writing first, and later printing, not only learned to transcribe the spoken word, but almost always, and almost always from the start, succeeded in producing hieroglyphics, ideograms, syllables, and letters which were unfailingly beautiful in design—regardless of their diversity—is certainly another reason for admiring this invention.

Each of the scripts of which I have spoken, each of those, as well, about which I have not been able to speak (the *tifinagh* characters of the Tuareg, for example, or the Scandinavian branch-runes, tent-shaped or pointed runes, and the Siberian runes, etc.) fulfills man by offering him something with which to nourish his intelligence, at the same time satisfying the desire in him for perfect forms; and this is so, regardless of the writing material or the writing tool used.

Consider that individual who inscribed a ritual formula on a bronze cast in wax, or who carved the resistant stone with his chisel, or who hollowed out the soft clay with his engraving point, or whose stylus incised the impressionable wax, or who lightly touched a sheet of transparent paper with a brush dipped in ink—and with such deceptive effortlessness that the letters or characters of divergent aspects seem to have been formed naturally and as if inevitably, quite differently from those made with chalk on slate, with the goose quill on vellum or parchment, or with the ball point pen on the so-called "bouffant" (featherweight) paper of the flyleaf in a contemporary book. Just compare the letters I have just mentioned with those produced by drawing pens tracing an alphabet on a sheet of Canson.

Is it possible to think of a material upon which man did not write before the invention of paper? He wrote on the hard rock and the soft stone, on leather and on parchment, on cotton and on silk, on wooden tablets covered with linen, on bone and on ostracon, on birch bark and on papyrus, on the inner bark of eaglewood and also on the palm leaf and the leaf of the Latania, on copperplate and on lacquered cardboard. Nor am I forgetting those Chinese *Annals of the Bamboo Books*, the title of which, of course, indicates the material used.

And every imaginable tool was used to trace the characters: with the chisel on stone, and even with the fingernail or the finger tip on sand and dust; with engraving points or punches, with the stylus or stiletto; with reeds, feathers of all kinds of birds, sharpened sticks;

Latin "calligram."
Anglo-Saxon manuscript of the tenth century.

ODIE DILECTSMI

PISCISQUINOTIUSAPPELLATURSIQUIDITURAQUAMEXCIPIBE ASIGNO AQUARIO QVI LABO RANTEM
QUONDAMISIMSERUASSEXISTIMATUR PROQUOBENEFICIO AQUARIO ONITS CIS
ETPIUSFILIORUMDICUIBUSANTIDIXIMUSINTERASTRA COMTITUM ITAQUE
SYRICOMPLURESPISCISHOMESIANT ETEORUMSIMULACRA INAURATAPRO
DPISPENATIBUSCOLUNTDEHOCCELISFECSCRISITINIER HIEALIALEM ETANTAR
CICONCIRCULUMMEDIARICIOMCOLLOCATUS SPECTARIAT EXORTUMQUE
DETURINTERCAPRICORNUM ETAQUARIUM ORE IXCIPIENS AQUAM
QUAEPROFUNDITURABAQUARIOHIC OCCIDIT ORIENTECANCROB
ORITURAUTEMCUMPISCIBUSEDISTOMNINO STELLA S STELLAE XII
RUMDUODECIMEXINDEAVESTELLA
SOLITIQUEMDICEREPISCEMUOLUTURA
INTERIORCAPRICORNOVERSUC
ARAUSTRUM

STELLACANOPOS

Exinde australem solui quem dicere piscem
Uoluitur inferior capricorno versur ad lustrum
pistricem obseruans procul illi pascibur herent
Et prope conspicies experta nomine omnes
Inter pistricem et piscem quem diximus austri
Stellae subpedibus stratis radiantis Aquari
propter Aquarius obscurum dextra regionnem
Exiguo quistellarum candore niret eis
Immultis timens his duo latelumina fulgent
Unum submagnis pedibus cernetur aquari
Quod super est, galido delapsum flumine fontis
Spingeram super caudam pistricis adhesit
Hae tenues stellae perhibentur nomine Aquari
Hic aliae uolitur paruo cumlumine clare
Atque priora pedum subsunt uestigia magni
Arqui tenentis &obscurae sinenomine cedunt

TISCIS

metal pens with large nibs, steel pens with fine points (ah! those penny penpoints of our childhood!); with iridium-tipped gold nibs, with "lead" pencils; with pieces of chalk; with ink pencils; and, most recently, with those horrible ball point pens, and so on.

And in what direction have men not written? Vertically and from right to left, vertically and from left to right, horizontally and from left to right, horizontally and from right to left; or, yet again, boustrophedon-style, as the savants have so clumsily termed it, in the manner of oxen as they plow the furrows, that is: horizontally but alternately, one line from left to right and the next line from right to left, or, if you like, one from right to left and the next from left to right. And as the Easter Islanders did, the odd lines could be arranged from left to right, the even lines from right to left, but in such a way that this time the sign would be reversed, with the top down.

In certain cases, it is true, only custom can explain the arrangement of the script. Consisting as it does of ideograms, each of which is complete in itself, Chinese can be read as easily in any five of the six ways which I have indicated. Even though, throughout the centuries, the Chinese book was arranged in vertical columns read from right to left, beginning on the page which would be the last one for us, it was often printed in vertical columns from left to right without its qualities

Illuminated letter in the Lectionary of Montmajour. Eleventh century.

Marginal note in eleventh-century psalter.

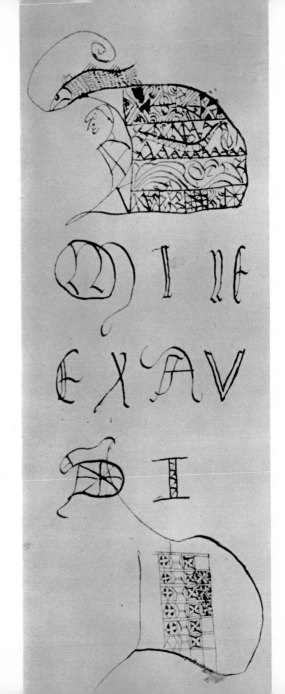

being at all affected. In the twentieth century, 60
and particularly since the Revolution, the
contemporary book is often arranged in horizontal lines which are read either from right
to left—in which case, the reading is begun
at what we call the "end" of the book—or, on
the contrary, in horizontal lines which are
read from left to right, so that nothing except
the characters themselves distinguishes the arrangement of Chinese printed material from
that of ours.

Without the tradition inherited from the
Chinese, the *kana* of the Japanese would be
written as naturally in horizontal lines from
left to right as in vertical columns from right
to left. And so, indeed, it happens that today
not only are the names of Western authors
transcribed in pure *kana* printed from left

From top to bottom:
Cursive upper case. Second century.
Cursive lower case. Third century.
Script used in pontifical missives.
    Fourth century.
Half-cursive roman. Seventh century.
Lombardo-Beneventine script.
    Eleventh century.
Half-uncial Irish. Eighth century.
Half-uncial Irish. Tenth century.
Carolingian lower case. Eighth century.
Carolingian upper case. Eighth century.
Carolingian lower case. Twelfth century.
Carolingian upper case. Twelfth century.
Gothic script of the chancelleries.
    Fourteenth century.
Humanist lower case. Fifteenth century.

French miniature of the fifteenth century.

1
2
3
4
5
6
7
8 君
9 君
10 君
11 長
12 兒
13 天
14 呂

to right on the title pages, but so are the titles in Chinese characters like 現代日本文學史 *History of Modern Japanese Literature,* even though the text of the book is arranged in the form of columns which are read from right to left.

Only our lazy minds invite us to think that the Latin alphabet commands us to read French, Spanish, Italian, or Portuguese from left to right. This very sentence can quite well be written from right to left with the same signs:

Onjy our lazy minds invite us to think that the Latin alphabet commands us to read French, Spanish, Italian, Portuguese from left to right.

No special study or preparation is necessary—all that is needed is a mirror—for anyone to read this apparent gibberish. With a brief training period, any schoolchild would be able to read without difficulty a French or English text printed in this way; it is the normally accepted arrangement of our books today which would then appear mysterious to them.

I could say as much about Arabic script; only habit makes us feel that this script is fated to be written from right to left. What is more, when it is recalled that the Etruscan alphabet, to take only one example, was at first written from right to left, according to the Semitic system and the Phoenician alphabet, before it was deciphered from left to right under the influence of the Latin alpha-

The lovers. *By the Master of the Book of Reason. Fifteenth century.*

bet, the obvious is no longer surprising: arbitrariness plays a great part in the arrangement of writing systems. Because of the long horizontal bar which follows almost uninterrup-

Gothic upper case. Sixteenth century.

tedly the line of the characters, I admit that the Brahmi script seems to demand the horizontal design. But I could just as well argue that, instead of being the cause of the horizontal design, this long stroke was a happy effect of it.

This characteristic of scripts is the most striking and at the same time the most misleading one: the direction in which they are written is most often the result of chance, tradition, or superstition.

More important is the writing material used,

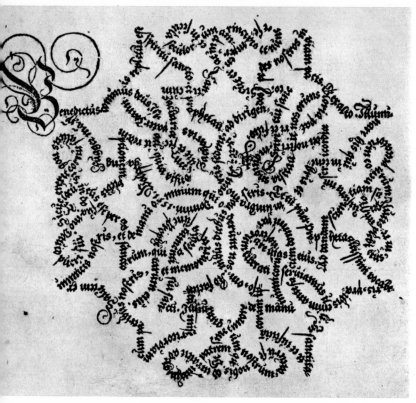

*Latin "calligram" in Gothic characters.
Sixteenth century.*

tually all wiped out in about the year 1200, at the time of the fire which ravaged the archives of Hattusa; they had been written on the most perishable of materials: tablets of wood covered with linen.

The writing material and the writing tool lend character to each of the scripts and seriously modify its nature. It is said that when ink and brush were first brought into use by General Mong-t'ien, since the brush could not write against the grain, many characters which particularly required reverse strokes could not survive this reform and were therefore replaced. Under the influence of paper which absorbed the ink from the brush, the heavy strokes and the contrasting hair lines which this instrument calls for were brought out again in Chinese characters.

Should it be said that they were brought out inevitably? That would be to oversimplify matters. With a quill pen, write a sentence cursively on a very smooth sheet of paper. Then, try to achieve the same *ductus,* as the savants put it, by cutting into granite. You will succeed, somehow, if you have infinite patience, but the result will not be natural, and I am not too sure that it would be beautiful. This is because the combination of a given writing surface and a given writing tool suggests certain forms of writing, perhaps even calls for them. It does not absolutely impose them, of course.

On the one hand, despite the many changes in writing materials and despite the sacred power attributed to writing by this or that civilization, some systems remained practically

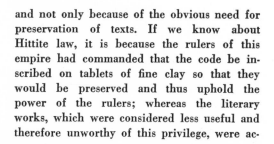

Portrait of Erasmus by Holbein.

and not only because of the obvious need for preservation of texts. If we know about Hittite law, it is because the rulers of this empire had commanded that the code be inscribed on tablets of fine clay so that they would be preserved and thus uphold the power of the rulers; whereas the literary works, which were considered less useful and therefore unworthy of this privilege, were ac-

Construction: Gothic lower case letters. Early seventeenth century.

unchanged; for instance, Egyptian hieroglyphics and Hebrew square letters. On the other hand, it often happens that even if he changes the writing material, man strives to conserve the outlines of a script influenced by the old material; thus, the first Greek papyri. And thus, also, our printed characters: the most highly perfected monotypes and linotypes reproduce, in the twentieth century, forms which had once been developed for the lapidary inscriptions of imperial Rome. And so the Chinese ink brush, running over the paper made of rice, of rag, or of the wild iris, fa-vored heavy strokes and hair lines; and certain stone carvers, enchanted by the beauty of these novel forms, transposed them onto their familiar material. It is notable that certain manuscript pages of the *Sseu-kou ts'iuan-chou* and certain inscriptions on stone present analagous characters, while, by a contrary influence, many calligraphers strive to achieve with their brushes forms analogous to those of Chinese lapidary workmanship.

More important, perhaps, than the writing material or the tracing implement is the social, political, and religious function of writing itself. From the good-for-nothing fellow who sneakingly scribbles his obscene pictographs on the walls of public "conveniences," let us turn to those Egyptian scribes in the Valley of the Kings who achieved perfection ornamenting at their leisure with adulatory inscriptions or sacred formulas the eternal resting places which the Pharaohs were having prepared for them during their lifetime. And to that functionary who copied bulls or private letters in the offices of pontifical chancelleries for the benefit of the princes of this world or the dignitaries of the Church. Do you suppose that he wrote characters resembling those, for example, of the twentieth century Parisian student in an overcrowded lecture room who hurriedly jots down the notes which he just manages to get as the magisterial lecturer reels them off at top speed? And this writing goes on while the student is standing, back or stomach to the wall, with his elbows stuck to his sides.

And is it to be supposed that our medieval writer-monks or, in Vedic India, the Brahmins who monopolized writing would have accepted the kinds of writing which satisfy our more or less democratic civilizations in which everyone is supposed to know how to write? Remember how many hours it took us in primary school, tongues stuck out studiously, merely to scrawl a blur of round hand or Gothic script, and how far we were from the perfection we admired on the manuscripts copied by the professionals? Already we have more than a presentiment that the typewriter will contribute grievously to the degeneration

Gothic upper case. Seventeenth century.

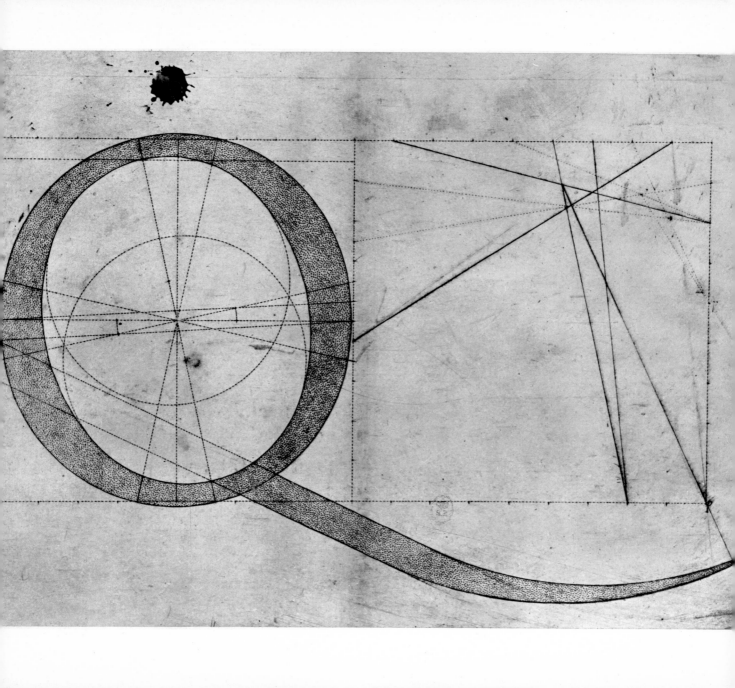

in quality of the individual's handwriting. Most people already do not know how to read a cursive letter, and even certain printers, accustomed as they are to receiving typed subject matter, commit many reading errors if they are entrusted with a manuscript the least bit difficult.

In *Arts et Métiers Graphiques*, I have read that "the invention of a character" in printing "can be as important in its effects as a new motor fuel." The anonymous author of this proposition appears to me to be somewhat biased. Brand-new though it may be, has Peignot type really changed our lives and revolutionized the French economy, as has gasoline, for instance, or electricity? I would not swear to that. But I recognize that it is worthwhile to examine the evolution of writing methods, if only to admire the skill of men in taking advantage of the utilitarian by transmuting it into a thing of beauty. Is there a cultivated man whose heart does not beat more quickly before a stele inscribed in precise cuneiforms; or before an inscription in the phallic Ammon temple recently excavated and reconstructed at Karnak; before a dalle, or slab, with Chinese classics carved on stone and now on view at Si-ngan-fou; a page printed by Gutenberg; or a line of the *Rig-Veda* in exquisite Brahmi?

How moving it is, for example, to follow in their successive graphic formations the stages of a Chinese character! Take the one which we now write 君, pronounced *kiun*, and which means, the prince. In *kou-wen*, the oldest writing known, this ideogram has tra-

Geometric construction of a capital Q.
Beginning of seventeenth century.

ditionally been analyzed in this way: a horned headdress, two arms, and a mouth. Father Wieger, who uses the official etymology, interprets thus: majesty, legislative power, and the executive power. Starting with form Number 4 of the illustration on page 62, notice the change: a scribe has transformed the headdress, and an aberrant character appears which is perpetuated in symbol Number 5. Later, a lazy scribe simplified one of the hands and transformed it into one simple stroke, which gives us aberrant character Number 6, which Li-Sseu, the minister of Ts'in Che Houng Ti (221-210 B.C.), interprets like this in the official index of characters: "hand which rules the people, mouth which legislates." And this is how character Number 7, called *siao tchouan*, which is classical writing, became stabilized. From this *siao tchouan* came Numbers 8 and 9 which are simply current ways of writing, called *li-tseu*. Now, the ink brush appears, with its bold and hairline strokes, and we have character Number 10. A system of ligatures and simplifications produced the cursives 11, 12, 13, 14, the first of which is called in Chinese a *lien-pei-tseu*; the others, *ts'ao-tseu*.

Thus, we clearly see how a script evolved, in conformity with the writing tool used, and how it always remained beautiful. Certain historians who write about China believe that at the time when writing was done on bamboo slats, the signs were traced with a hollow reservoir tube made of bamboo; the flow of the ink, regulated by a wick, could be arrested by blocking the upper orifice. In whatever direction, then, the writing instrument moved, it could produce neither the bold nor the hairline strokes. When Tch'eng Miao invented a kind of tapering wooden pencil to be dipped into a varnish for writing on silk, the circular contours of the ancient characters inevitably became squares and the curves were broken into angular designs. The brush concluded this evolution. Anyway, regardless of their variations, the fourteen forms which the character *kiun* took in four millenniums at least have this in common: they are beautiful.

This is what Victor Ségalen says in his preface to *Stèles*: "How could their writing not be beautiful? So close to original forms (a man under the roof of heaven—an arrow winging toward the sky—a horse, mane flying in the wind, legs poised for action—three mountain peaks—the heart and its auricles, and the aorta), the characters do not allow for either ignorance or clumsiness. Whatever pictures human beings see through the human eye, pictures which pass through the muscles, the fingers, and other instruments of the human nervous system, must necessarily undergo some distortion; it is in this way that art penetrates science. Today merely correct, the Chinese characters were full of distinction at the time of Yong-Tcheng; elongated under the Ming, in the elegant shape of garlic cloves; classic under the T'ang; full and vigorous under the Han; and going back still farther to the nude curved symbols, curved as elemental things are curved."[1] Go to a Chinese

[1] Early Han: 206 B.C.-9 A.D.; Late Han: 25-200 A.D.; T'ang: 618-907; Ming: 1368-1644; Yong-Tcheng, Emperor of the Ts'ing or Manchu dynasty (1644-1911), reigned in the eighteenth century (born in 1677, he ascended the throne in 1723 and died in 1736).

The schoolmaster. *Seventeenth century.*
Engraving by Abraham Bosse.

Lettre flamende

eele naer het oude spreeckwoort, niet willende te spreken en kunnen nochtans niet swijgen: Ende willen leerende seif hiren dy se selfe niet verstaen, oide het selue aen anderen wijsmaeckende nemen sij aen den naem van geleert te weesen, sijnde aldus mee meesters van de ongeleerde als discipulen van de doctoren. b , q , v , ʒ .

Het gheleert dat iemant is h en ir wordt lauw een groote ourwen hij sijn sij willen leeren anders dy baetter is als hij.

a,b,c,d,e,f,g,h,i,k,l,m,n,o,v,q,r,s,t,u,v,w,x,y,z .

A B C D E F G H K L M O p q

R S T W B Y Z .

Barbedor

restaurant today; written with a ball point pen, the characters on your menu have once again lost their bold and delicate shading, and also their beauty.

With so little space to tell their story, how is it possible to follow the development of those beautiful—or nearly always beautiful—forms which man was able to create in his principal writing systems? If we follow the hieroglyphics to the hieratic writing; the seals or maybe even the demotic; or if we go from the square Hebrew letters to the rabbinical scripts, what beautiful stories we find, and true ones, too! Stiff and angular when inscribed on stone or metal, Arabic script very soon became more rounded and more sinuous as soon as it was written on papyrus.

Since I have chosen to point out the evolution of a Chinese ideogram, perhaps it is a good idea now for me to examine the changes which the Latin alphabet has undergone in the course of its adventuring. How clear and legible it already was, this Roman lapidary script of the second century before our era: all in capitals, without heavy or hairline strokes, or any linkage whatsoever. With Trajan's inscription of the first century A.D., there appeared, seemingly accomplished once and for all, other capitals which were at first traced on stone with heavy and hairline strokes and connections; these were to define until our time the norms of our alphabet.

About the same time, the Romans produced

Flemish letters by Barbedor.
Seventeenth century.

German engraving of the seventeenth century.

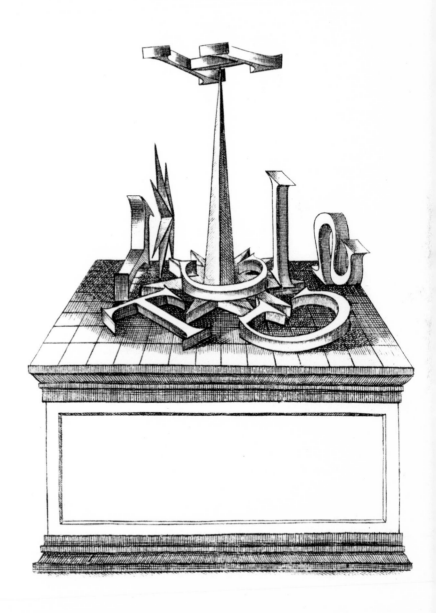

the *capitalis quadrata,* or square capitals. The expert can recognize in these the predominant characteristics of the lapidary inscriptions of Trajan, but accentuated by the movement of the edged reed or the quill pen held in a nearly horizontal position in relation to papyrus or parchment.

As happens to all scripts, and as if already time meant money to man, the Roman scribe soon simplified this writing he had inherited, from which emerged the *rustica,* our rustic capital, and the Roman uncial; these have been tremendously satisfying as far back as the most ancient forms from which they came (in the inscriptions of Timgad). Both of these are polished scripts, and calligraphic, but simplified though they were acknowledged to be, both were unsuitable for rapid writing.

Concurrently with this evolution of lapidary Roman, we note the appearance of a cursive script, cursive because of its having been written with a stylus on a wax-coated tablet, or perhaps it was due to the sliding of the pen on the surface of papyrus. In conformity with one or another writing material, with one or another writing tool, scripts adopted angular or supple forms. Already, certain letters were ascending above the others, but this did not happen with the capitals, thus preparing the way for the distinction which we take for granted today, but which was not made from the start between what we call our capitals and our small letters. As beautiful as they were legible, the Roman capitals gratify the mind and the eye. If the capitals in cursive

Numerals. English engraving of the eighteenth century.

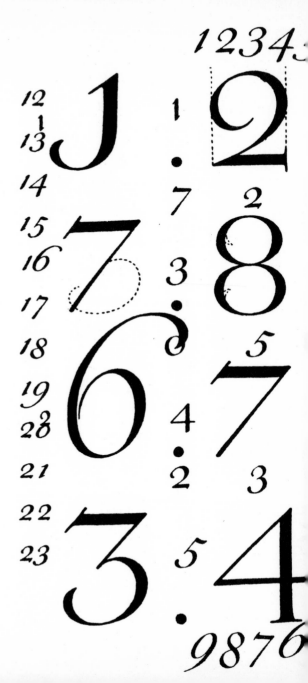

6 7 8 9 0 1 2 3 4 5 6 7 8 9 0 1 2 3 4

3 .3 .4 .5 .6
3 4 5 6
5 9 6 0 8 1 4 2 24
25
1 .2 .3 .4 .5 26
5 6 7 8 27
0 7 8 9 2 6 3 28
29
8 .9 .1 .2 .3 30
7 5 6 4 31
4 2 0 3 7 5 32
33
3 .2 7 .3 9 .4 8 .7 5 34
35

5 4 3 2 1 3 5 2 6 4 5 6 4 2 0 9 Shelley.

script fatigue the eye, what then can be said for cursive small letters? Whereas someone who knows Latin can without much study successfully grapple with a rustic or uncial inscription, he risks being baffled for a long time, if not for good, before these down strokes, these oblique strokes, and these ligatures which compose the minuscule cursive. It goes without saying that in this type of script, the writing style of each scribe imparts a rather personal touch to the writing. Awkward though it may appear to us, this script, nevertheless, is not less important to us than the lapidary Roman because, if we owe to the latter the design of our capitals, Western writing hardly owes less to the cursive small letter. The Christians readily wrote in uncials, but they did not neglect the cursive minuscule from which they gradually obtained the half-uncial.

No less than the fall of the Roman Empire, the development of Christianity certainly plays its role in the history of our alphabet. As Roman civilization was disintegrating, writing styles tended to become diversified while the differences diminished between book or library writing and that of the chancelleries; the uncial and the half-uncial tended to become specialized for liturgical and religious writing. Without minimizing the Lombard script (which some prefer to call the Italian hand) or the Visigothic (what prestige the school of Toledo had in the ninth century!), it was the Irish and Frankish scripts which spread and oriented the writing styles of the Christian West.

Johann Sebastian Bach:
Cantata, Nun komm, der Heiden Heiland.

So intertwined, however, is the history of these scripts, that certain characteristics of Visigothic writing are recognized to be almost like those of our Merovingian, and even, in

Composing room.
Engraving in the Encyclopédie.

certain respects, of the Carolingian. But the supremacy of the Carolingian over all of its contemporary scripts ought not to surprise us today: for a script to be a successful one, it is not enough that it be written quickly; it is just as necessary for it to read well. Those who designed the alphabets realized that a good part of the pleasure that a script offers us is a reward for our laziness; the less effort it requires of us, the better and the more

beautiful we judge it to be. But neither the script of the Merovingian legal writing nor the Irish half-uncials indulge our laziness.

In spite of its name, it would be naive to think that Carolingian sprang fully formed from a decision of Charlemagne. We know now that the Irish monk Alcuin had nothing to do with it either. Quite simply, from among the scripts not yet stabilized then, Charlemagne had enough taste to choose the best and enough authority to impose its use. When he ordered that all existing literature in his time be rewritten in this style, he diffused it all over Christian Europe. We should not forget those monks of Aix-la-Chapelle and of Autun, of Corbie and of Tours, who, before the Edict of 789, had reinvented the new forms; that is to say, the ancient forms. It is to them, above all, that we owe the Carolingian. To disengage itself entirely from the Merovingian tradition and to regain a good part of the vigor and simplicity it had known in Rome, this script needed nearly a century. Inspired by the *rustica* and the uncial, Carolingian shows that Charlemagne felt himself to be and, indeed, desired to be considered the heir of the Roman emperors. In another way, too, it became clear that he wished to be acknowledged their successor: his reign was also the one in which certain abbreviations again became widespread; the Roman equivalent of these had been those "Tironian notes" which had existed since the days of the Republic and been used in the offices of the Empire. With us, stenography is the closest equivalent.

From a French treatise on writing.
Seventeenth century.

In the twelfth and thirteenth centuries, Western writing underwent a change. This is a good time to assess once again the little we surely know and to note how many questions

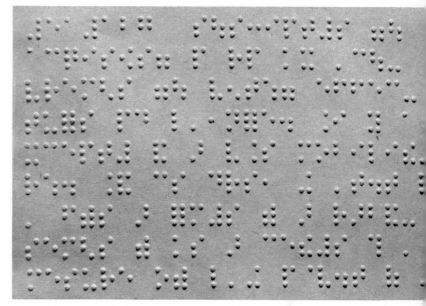

Braille writing.

remain open about the history of our alphabet alone. It is impossible, for instance, to form an idea of what this revival was without having studied, among other works, that of Istvàn Hajnal on the teaching of writing in the medieval universities, an edition of which, thoroughly revised and enlarged by Laszlo Mezey, was published in Budapest in 1959 by the publishing house of the Academy of Science. Until the treatise of Hajnal appeared, historians of Western writing and paleographers generally supported the idea that book or library writing was taught in the *scriptoria* of the churches; legal writing, in chancery guilds. The Hungarian expert claims, on the contrary, that during this critical and revolu-

Etiquette-rebus for candy box.
French engraving of the nineteenth century.

tionary period of Western graphiology, the unity of the writing, evident to him, may be explained by a fact contested until then; namely, that the universities were at that time "the central regulatory establishments for writing usage" and that the "forms which developed there were spread all over Europe,"

notably from the *Studium* of Paris, to which Hajnal attributes a directing role.

This much at least appears to be conceded: while the Irish monks started from the Roman cursive and developed a script which prevailed in the British Isles until the thirteenth century and which, toward the end of its evolution seemed to be searching unsuccessfully for the norms of what we call Gothic writing, the Carolingian, which had replaced Irish writing on the Continent, substituted for the reign of the horizontal a predominant vertical characteristic and for the semicircular curve of the Roman arch, the "breaks" of the Gothic arch. The angular design of this script became more marked as the letters became narrower. From France, the new writing spread across Europe in the thirteenth century, thus seeming to confirm Hajnal's theory.

Since a page of Gothic makes one think of a chain or of the weave in cloth, it was soon to be called *textura*. It is not because this new script was as precise or as legible as the Roman square writing that it attracted stubborn partisans, even much later on, but because of its ornamental character. The Victorian age made whimsical use of it. With a square-nibbed pen, people of my age had to suffer in primary school over the broken strokes of Gothic.

From Gothic, in its turn, was constructed a cursive, slightly inclined to the right, but clearly inspired by *textura,* upon which, in its turn, it was going to react: it is in this way that so-called bastard writings were developed

The schoolteacher.
Drawing by a seven-year-old child.

i cr ? C ? d zéro , a . B : x n a ooooooo

g 2 fois 100 = 200 j x + o eau l'institutrice ?

☒ ☒ 7 v e : au l. x

4 D d 123 au 4 0 + e

t o a k Bien + très mal

2 3 y f g A - ui qui que 8 t f.

O O u y M a qui que 7 vu

oui A B quoi ?

o x R 4 non CP

k A Z Z 5 x v v t : E B R i

+ silence ! dire hi hi an 9 58 2001 f l 1 FOIS 6 = 6

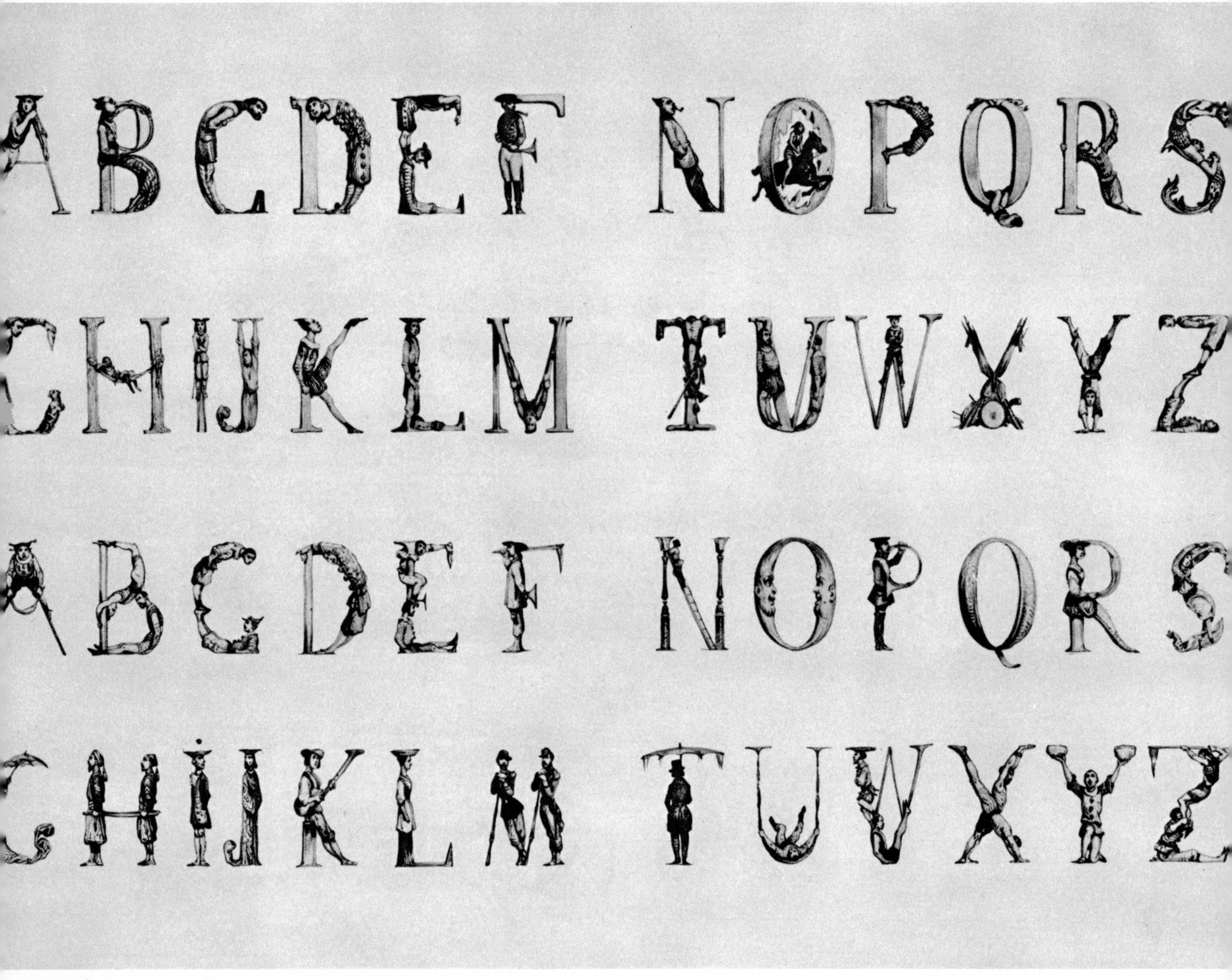

and diffused and, according to circumstances, sometimes approached the cursive, sometimes *textura*.

When Gutenberg at last invented printing with movable letters in Europe, he chose alphabets closely related to the *textura* of the most beautiful manuscripts. From the start, he attained perfection. However evident the merits of Schwabacher (fifteenth century) may be to us, this letter which certainly pleases the eye, but which rather obviously admits its bastardization, does not give as much satisfaction as a page of the Bible. Such, apparently, are the merits of this letter which we call "Gothic,"—the Germans call it *die Fraktur* —that it has been perpetuated in Germany to this day, as much for the printing of books as for newspapers.

Observing as we do that the handwritten scripts and the alphabets created for typography follow in their large outlines the evolution of intellectual and artistic values (Charlemagne imposing a script of Roman origin; Gothic architecture projecting itself, so to speak, in miniature, in the alphabet of the same name), we are hardly surprised to discover that Italy, rebellious toward architectural Gothic, transformed Gothic writing to suit her own taste, perhaps softened it, certainly rounded it, and originated in the fifteenth century, *rotunda*, our Gothic round hand.

Almost insanely in love with Greek culture, the humanists did not want to stop there. Goths, Visigoths, Ostrogoths were so many

"Fanciful" alphabet.
French lithograph of the nineteenth century.

Vandals or barbarians, as far as they were concerned, who had ruined Roman civilization. Just as, a little later on, our classical seventeenth century was to hope that the

Rotary press introduced at the International Exposition of 1878.

cathedrals would be destroyed, the Italian humanists condemned the Gothic letter. Reacting against the slender columns and the verticality of a civilization abominable to them, they rediscovered the horizontal in

Z

Greek architecture and imposed it on the script. In Carolingian writing, they discerned what it truly was, a tribute to the Roman Empire. It is ironical that Gothic itself also

Poem by Guillaume Apollinaire: composition in 48-point Elzevir foundry type.

derives from the Carolingian and consequently from Romanism; but that is the way of men, wavering like drunkards, never knowing which step comes first—as Montaigne pointed out. There is nothing more delightfully impure, in one sense, than this humanist script which, in the selfsame line of writing, associates capitals inspired by a lapidary alphabet with small letters whose ancestry leaves no room for doubt and can be traced back to the Carolingian or Caroline minuscule, which was definitely not incised in stone, but traced on it. But in spite of this mixed breeding, the marriage of the humanistic majuscule and minus-

cule was not such an unhappy one! Not only does humanistic typography still dominate our printing cases, but the script is still alive, even in our primary schools, with some changes, of course, as in italics. The latter is a cursive script derived from the humanist, which spread rather suddenly in the sixteenth century. Rather strongly inclined toward the right, at an angle of 8 degrees and sometimes 10 degrees, the rounds tend toward the oval, the stems lengthen, the letters are closer together and are connected.

So successful was it that the printers imitated it. To Aldus Manutius is generally attributed the idea of establishing the first alphabets of what we have called since then *italics,* although more than one typography specialist prefers to name this character according to its function: the *cursive.* Here are a few dates to serve as landmarks for its success. Whereas in 1509, the book of Luca Pacioli, *De Divina Proportione,* and, sixteen years later, the celebrated treatise of Albert Dürer were establishing the norms of the Roman capital letter, Ludovico Arrighi had defined, as early as 1522, those of the cursive, our italics, in: *Il modo e regola de scrivere littera corsiva,* the methods and rules of writing cursive letters. Less than a half-century later, this technique conquered France; it is demonstrated in the book of Jacques de la Rue: *Exemplaires de plusieurs sortes de lettres,* samples of several kinds of letters. In 1571, it was England's turn in: *A Book Containing Diverse Sortes of Handes,* by Jehan de Beauchesne and John Baildon. Several years later,

Lower case letter in Elzevir type.

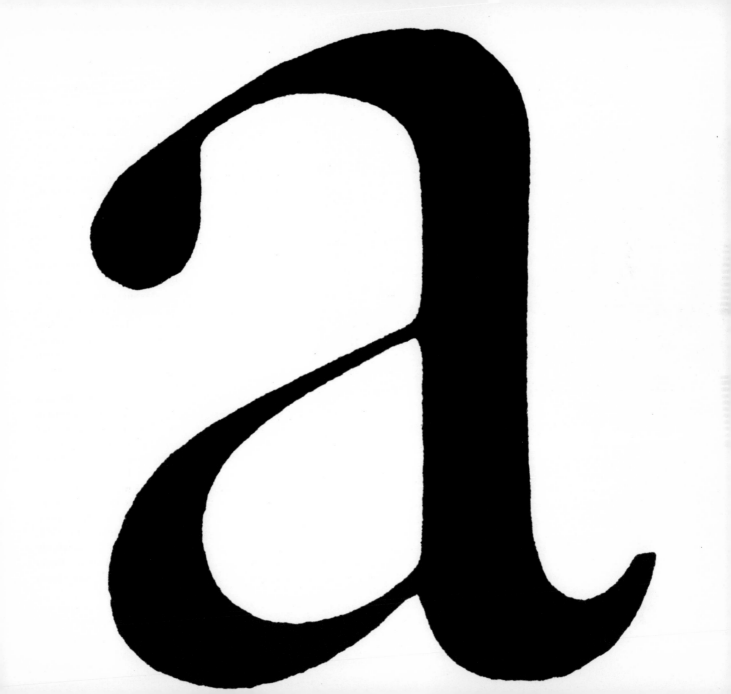

in 1577, Francisco Lucas brought it to Spain in his *Art de Escrebir,* the art of writing. But already, and as early as 1550, Italy had abandoned the cursive for the printing of books

Engraved advertisement for typewriters. England. Beginning of the twentieth century.

and had reserved it for marginal notes, titles, and quotations, words to which it was desired to attract the attention of the reader.

The writing of the seventeeth century cannot hide its debt to humanistic cursive. As the technique of copperplate engraving, which allows, at need, an extremely delicate hairline stroke, was gaining ground then in Europe and was inspiring the printers, characters in which the hairline strokes of the cursive were accentuated to the maximum degree were created and cast for printing. Although this technique did not a priori seem to suit printing very well, it caught on, and Walbaum, Didot, and Bodoni were originated.

Inevitably, this classic script engendered, in its turn, its cursive, from which our scripts are derived, at least those which were taught at the beginning of the century: the fine metal penpoint favored the alternation of heavy and fine strokes. With the ball point pen, shading is lost; the bold and fine strokes tend to disappear; while the line is being written, it is being engraved, so to speak, on the paper.

It is impossible to list all those who have left their mark on the modern and contemporary history of writing or typography. However, at least to recall that they belonged to different nations, let us cite some names: Robert Estienne, Elzevir, Plantin, Garamont, Caslon, van de Velde, Baskerville, Ibarra, Morris, von Larisch, Weiss, Peignot, Jacno.

I am not forgetting Barbedor. As if trying to justify his florid name, he unfortunately was not a stranger to that baroque writing which enjoyed something of a vogue in the second half of the seventeenth century, with its extravagant heavy strokes and its immoderate stems. This style, nevertheless, survived into the eighteenth century. It was then that the horrors began.

Under the combined influence of universal

Three-ruble banknote. Russia. 1905.

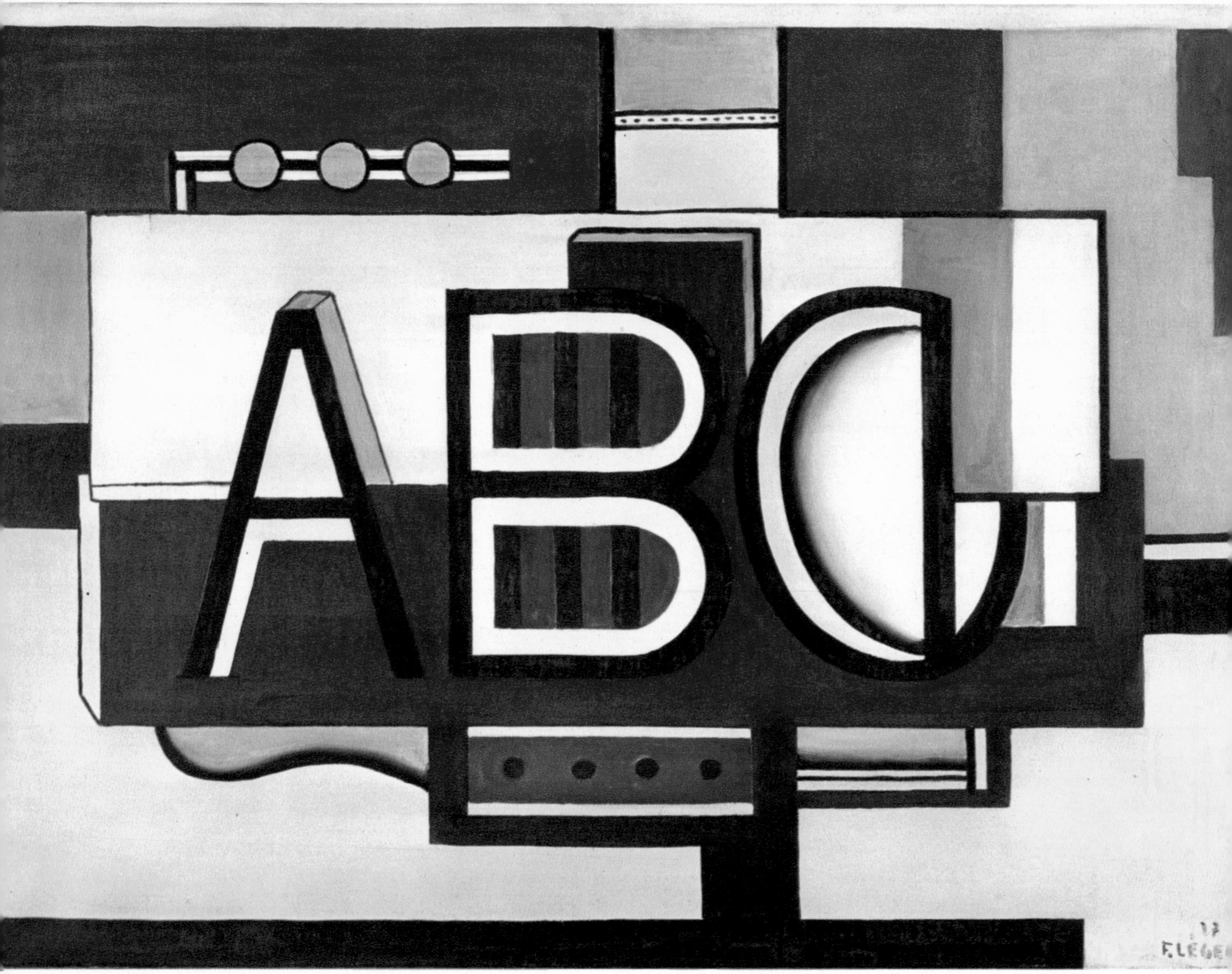
ABC
17
F.LÉGE

education and commercial publicity, a vulgar ornamentation encumbered the alphabets of the nineteenth century with flourishes, doubled the lines of their letters, distended them like hernias, shaded them with crosshatchings, elongated them, flattened them, stretched them, thickened them. Alas, what had happened to the beautiful initials of our old manuscripts? In the twentieth century, it is no longer a question of gratifying the spirit and resting the eye. In every possible way—and usually it is the worst way—the aim is to force the attention of the masses. The capital letters of what is called "la belle époque" ("the grand period") in France were sometimes as loaded with nude women as were the pictures of the academic painters of the Third Republic. Today, every businessman wants for his signboard or his product some indication which will distinguish it from the signboard or product of the next fellow. This is how the emulation of bad taste flourishes. No one hesitates now to compose a title in as many different types as there are letters in the words. To seduce, or rather, to violate the attention, everything is put out of line in relation to the horizontal.

Out of this vulgarity emerged Egyptian, Antique, and Peignot.

And, finally, at the end of the line, we hear of "New Wave scripts." Now, the letter in relief has appeared and the latest metamorphosis, to my knowledge, of the myth of Rimbaud, "ultra-letters in their savage state."

Fernand Léger: Still life. *1927.*

Alphabet for deaf-mutes. Spanish engraving of the seventeenth century.

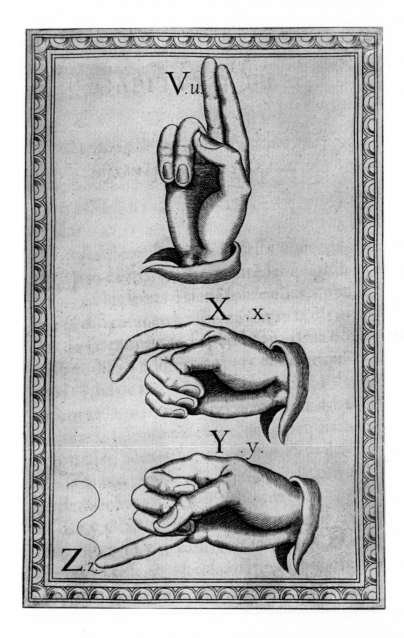

I cite the press release of a recent work printed in ultra-letters, *Hépérile éclaté*:

"Writing did not await our intervention to burst forth.

Henri Michaux: Signs. *1951.*

"There are ultra-letters in a savage state. Our merit — or our astuteness — is to have perceived ultra-letters where we were accustomed to seeing distorted letters.

"And, finally, we use webs of fluted glass to rid written words of their significance."

In this latest avatar of the Latin alphabet, what a superb illustration we have of that universal nihilism which, quite as much as —or perhaps more, alas, than—universal relativity, will mark the twentieth century, and of which Hitler's concentration camps apparently have not exhausted the horror. Since Charlemagne, who wanted to build a world, revived the Roman capital letter, it is natural that our time, which can only think of apocalypses, should insist first of all upon destroying writing and afterwards discovering the cost of its folly. How do these ultra-letter theorists plan to use their webs of fluted glass in dealing with an SOS signal transmitted by Morse Code? And do they intend, perhaps, ingeniously to blur under the fingers of the blind the Braille writing invented for them?

Before ultra-letters, I admit, there were all sorts of typographical eccentricities: alphabets worthy of Arciboldo and parentheses by Raymond Roussel; nor is Mallarmé to be forgotten. Thanks to Raymond Queneau, we even know about the "cracked" typographer, Nicolas Cirier, with his *typographical eye* and his *Apprentif ɹnǝʇɐɹʇsᴉuᴉɯp∀:*

"The indignation of the persecuted, the exaltation of the paranoiac can no more be expressed by capital letters or marks indicating

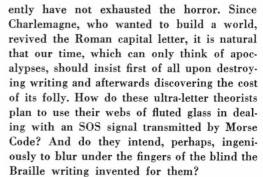

Marinetti: Words, in futurist style. *1919.*

Pages 92/93. Signatures: 1. *Philip the Good.* 2. *Corneille.* 3. *Louis XI.* 4. *Titian.* 5. *Bonaparte.* 6. *Captain Cook.* 7. *Maximilian I, emperor of Germany.* 8. *Francis Jammes.* 9. *Benjamin Franklin.* 10. *Ronsard.* 11. *Richard III of England.* 12. *Paul Klee.* 13. *Madame de Sévigné.* 14. *Louis XIII of France.* 15. *Oscar Wilde.* 16. *Charles-Quint.* 17. *Ezra Pound.* 18. *Maréchal Ney.* 19. *Erik Satie.* 20. *Catherine de Médicis.* 21. *Gustave III of Sweden.* 22. *Victor Hugo.* 23. *Mozart.* 24. *Goya.* 25. *George Washington.* 26. *Guillaume Budé.*

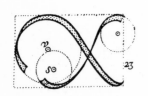

1

2 Cornwall

3

4 Titiano Pittore

5 Bonaparte

6 Sam Hook

7

8

9 B Franklin

10 Ronsard

11

12 K

13

14 Louis
je men vas à la chasse

ellipsis than the authors already cited; and the cosmogonic conceptions of schizophrenics are of such a bizarre nature that they could never, to my knowledge, at least, break through the rigor of the Gutenberg laws of composing type. Therefore, our investigation would have had singularly and paradoxically poor results if by chance (which is really not chance since it is precisely by chance that we wanted to come upon it) we had not found a printer among the literary madmen." See opposite. As a social symptom, this was not so serious as the so-called ultra-letters which annihilate writing itself.

This desire to disfigure the signs and to despoil writing of its function—how is it that it is manifesting itself at the precise moment when Western art criticism is interpreting in terms of "calligraphy" an important segment, and not one to be scorned, of contemporary painting?

At the beginning of an article on precisely these affinities between calligraphy and the art of Soulages, Tobey, and Hartung, Jean-François Revel cites a remark of Malraux: Before a painting of Mathieu, Malraux is said to have celebrated the birth, belated, but nevertheless the birth, of a Western "calligrapher." Assuming that the use of this word is legitimate here, we must say that Mathieu is far from the position where he might be considered our leading calligrapher. About Georges Braque, it has been written that two of his works in which he uses plaster on a black background constitute "one of the peaks of calligraphic art." Furthermore, that individual discerns in Arp "the accent of the oriental ideogram; the humorous touches of the Chinese character ennoble the *Apparat d'une danse....* These novel compositions are kinds of autonomous letters." Wishing to elucidate the *Women with Undone Hair Greeting the Crescent Moon* that Miro painted August 24, 1939, here are the analogies which Raymond Queneau finds: "That these are women is not to be doubted—they are wearing dresses. (On one of these women, the one facing us, the breasts are indicated.) And, besides, they are identical to the Chinese key 女 , we note, which means woman. The crescent moon in this painting is symbolized by the woman's classic face (but it is not 'white'). The picture, then, is constructed on the following graphic scheme:

女
女 女

...and if I have utilized the resemblance between the symbolic figure of the woman and the corresponding Chinese character, it is not for nothing, but rather because the painting of Miro is a script one must know how to decipher."

Well before these artists, Paul Klee, between 1916 and 1918, undeniably influenced by the arts of the Far East, composed several poem-pictures, the almost illegible text of which merged with his colored squares. Towards 1930, this same artist, inspired this time by Arabic script, painted various liana or creepers, so-called "vegetal ideograms." However close to ideograms they may be, they are not ideograms because they obviously have no meaning. And before Mathieu, there were

Mark Tobey: Calligraphic structure. 1958.

the paintings of Michaux in which familiarity with China is expressed in "graphisms" which a superficial appraisal might readily call "calligraphic."

Saul Steinberg: Design.

Assuming that words should have meaning, all of these works are neither more nor less calligraphic than those drawings composed of one continuous stroke which were popular in the eighteenth century or those that are still favored in the United States among certain so-called primitives. We might as well designate as calligraphy the "calligrammes" of Apollinaire, in which the more or less poetic phrase outlines and signifies the object that is being suggested, at one and the same time.

Important as it is for us to welcome the

spread of enlightenment, it is just as vital for us to deplore the misinterpretation of the arts of Asia. This misapprehension leads us to confuse Chinese or Arabic calligraphy with contemporary pursuits which should not be compared with this calligraphy at all.

Consider Claudel, for instance, who says in spite of the fact that he lived for some years in the Far East: "The principle of the Roman Letter was the vertical line; the essential characteristic of the Chinese character appears to have been the horizontal." Besides the fact that this proposition runs counter to the historical study of the Roman alphabet (*capitalis quadrata* says very much better what it was), it has nothing to do with the Chinese ideograms, as even a slight analysis of their evolution would show. It is a known fact that in certain scripts, the *Li-tseu* particularly, some calligraphers sought the horizontal. Victor Ségalen admires with great sensitivity its "robustness" and "horizontal equilibrium"; but Chinese script and calligraphy have varied so very much in the course of the millenniums! It would be better to read Souen Kouo-t'ing in his treatise *On Writing*:

"Obviously, everything changes with time, and writing cannot escape from this rule. When the customs of a people change, it is natural and logical that the way of writing change also." If one were to seek, for example, a script, among all the others, which avoids the horizontal, there is the rapid and graceful *ts'ao chou* which, throughout the centuries, inspired and frustrated Chinese calligraphers.

Graffiti.

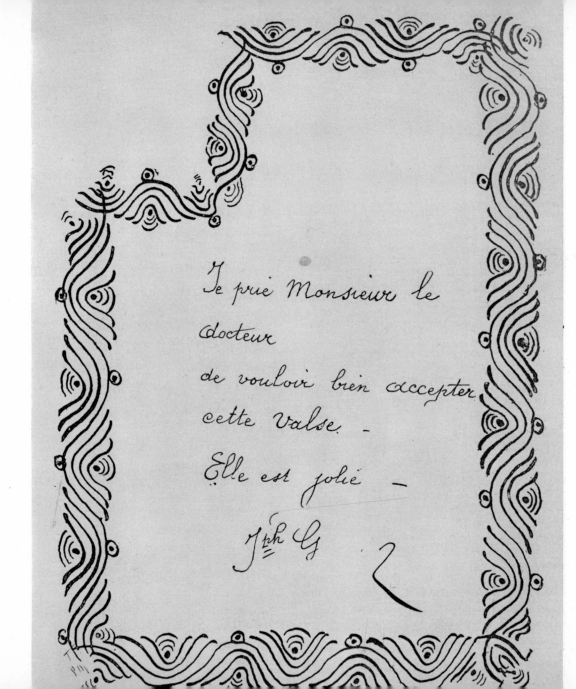

Je prie Monsieur le

docteur

de vouloir bien accepter

cette Valse. -

Elle est jolie -

Jph G

99 It is a pity that instead of knowledge about Islam or China, we have the vaticinations of our present-day critics and the "pursuits" of our painters which betray the malaise of merely signs"; in other words, a writing system "entirely cerebral, spare, and without an enveloping aura." Of course, in this statement he movingly informs us of his repugnance for

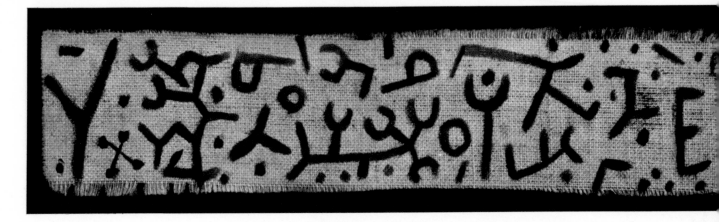

Paul Klee: Writing. *1940.*

our times and the obsessions of our artists. In certain frescoes of Bamyan, many of the mouths he draws look like those typographical signs which are known as "braces." When Malraux analyzes these, he claims that "this calligraphy is not an accident." In doing so, he is simply confusing, like nearly everyone else today, calligraphic art with mere design.

To Egyptian script (which he judges to be "bestial and particularly childish"), Michaux a little too hastily opposes Chinese writing which "from the beginning showed no sensuous appeal in the style of the writing, but

Letter written and decorated by an invalid beset by a persecution mania.

sensuousness, but he is totally mistaken about calligraphy. Although Egyptian script did not evolve toward the same kind of abstraction as the Chinese did, was it not, in more than one sense, infinitely more abstract since, detached from a meaningful image, it conceived phonetic notation and paved the way for an alphabet? The truth is that for Michaux the representational aspect of hieroglyphic characters evokes an art which it is the fashion to belittle today. To call a writing system bestial only because the sign of a pintail duck in flight can easily be recognized in a hieroglyph is, of course, ingenious, but rather silly. All that it proves is, according to the analysis of Jean Capart in his *Propos sur l'art égyptien*, remarks on Egyptian art, that "the art of writing was not different from the art of design" at the time of the Pharaohs; "sometimes, on the same tomb, one finds an animal represented simultaneously as it actually looks and flashes or like falling rocks. There are signs inclined like flying birds or galloping beasts. Characters look like dancing phoenixes, like crawling serpents, like precipitous crags, like

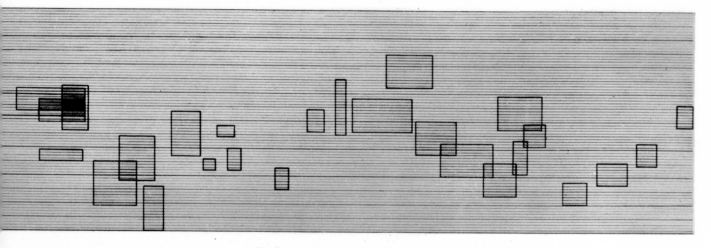

Karlheinz Stockhausen: Electronic Etude No. 2 *(fragment of score).*

as a writing sign: the two images are identical." But, contrary to the idea of Michaux, the same thing happened in China. The painter is a calligrapher and the calligrapher is a painter: so much so that current language associates calligraphy (*chou*) and painting (*houa*) in a phonic and logical complex, *chou-houa,* as demonstrative in its way as the expression with which the Chinese designate landscapes: *chan-chouei* (mountains-waters).

Let us take up again for a moment the treatise of Souen Kouo-t'ing. What a surprise awaits our calligraphy fanatics! "Among the great calligraphers may be found signs straight as hanging needles and marks round as dewdrops. One also finds signs jagged as lightning abrupt peaks. Some of them are as heavy as thick clouds; others are as light as the wings of cicadas. They are as enchanting as the moon appearing on the horizon, as splendid as stars suspended in the firmament."

Even the 8 strokes of which the beautifully traced characters are composed (8, according to some; 14, according to others; and 72, to anyone who carries analysis of form to an extreme degree) bear names evocative of images, objects, living beings: the falling dewdrop, the suspended needle, the orchid leaf, the golden knife, the hook in the shape of a dragon's tail, the hook in the shape of the floating swan, the sportive butterfly, the coiled dragon. Even the defects in badly written char-

101 acters are expressed by a vocabulary quite simply representational: beware the sign which shows the waist of the wasp! avoid the tail of a mouse! flee from the head of an ox! watch out for the broken branch! be careful of the leg of the stork! These are the admonitions of the perfect calligrapher in China.

And still there are people among us who write that "the practice of decorative calligraphy for such a long period of time had accustomed the 'Chinese' eye to estimate the virtues of a non-representational art." Here, first of all, the thesis is questionable because so many Chinese characters are strictly figurative, or representational: one represents a tree; one a door; one, the heart; one, a horse with its legs and its mane; one, a complete bird. Secondly, the thesis is blameworthy because all calligraphers profess that one of the rules of the art consists in tracing characters—however cursive they may seem—which evoke in our imagination living forms or inanimate objects. Contemplating the carefully drawn character *yi* [*yee*] of his name, Chiang Yee, author of a fine treatise entitled *Chinese Calligraphy*, expressed wonder about the character which actually means "constant rule," but resembles a stork standing on one of its legs, looking stable, of course, yet in a state of balance, poised for movement. This same author forthwith deplores the fact that one cannot always find "representations which correspond exactly to the characters"; but he confirms the fact that at least this rule is followed: "Every carefully drawn character

Camille Bryen: Hépérile éclaté.
Ultra letters.

must be as well-proportioned as a human being, an animal, a plant, or an object, whatever it may be, surprised in movement."

If, then, our abstract or non-objective painters are enchanted by Chinese calligraphy, it is through a total misconception of the aims of an art which, having started by being representational, requires a return to representation in another form. Even in the details of its technique, Chinese calligraphy uses the representational, the concrete — transfiguring and stylizing it, no doubt, but what artist has ever proceeded otherwise?

This is not all: for many of our painters and critics, calligraphy plays, in a way, the role that our symbolists attribute to free verse and our surrealists to automatic writing. They see in it a way of expressing their deepest feelings, and they seek in these so-called calligraphic contours a refuge, a return to the existential. To attain their aims, all they have to do is forget that every Chinese character— although it has some asymmetry, without which there can be no perfect beauty, in China or elsewhere—must, complementarily, be inscribed in a perfect square, divided, as the case may be, into two vertical rectangles or two horizontal rectangles, unless it is in four or nine equal squares. According to its components and proportions, then, each character must be inscribed in such a system of rectangles or such a complex of squares. Why, then, should these modern painters who seek individualistic expression mock at the old disciplines, like the mathematical "golden section," when they themselves are calling for a discipline — Chinese calligraphy — which im-

Neon signs.

poses laws at least as exacting as the series of Fibonacci?

Nor should those who strive for free self-expression forget the precision of the stroke in Chinese calligraphy which does not tolerate either re-doing or retouching, and without which, the writing would be only infantile scribbling. But, from Hartung to Soulages and from Tobey to Zao Wou-ki, I see men who are certainly familiar with Chinese or Japanese characters, but they are also painters who use their brushes to lay on big black dripping splashes or to make vague, broken wash drawings suggesting mannikins or robots, or even to outline scrawls of thin, wavering lines, retouched many times.

To discern in this sort of thing a technique analogous to calligraphy, it is necessary, I suggest, to drain the word *calligraphy* of everything which, until about 1960, determined its meaning.

Finally, and above all, our painters and critics have a genius for forgetting the essential: whether it be Arabic, Chinese, or Japanese, all calligraphic design has meaning and expresses a moral principle or poetic images. The most abstract of quadrangular Kufic writing, for those who do not know Arabic, may, I admit, evoke nothing but certain systems of lines related to some of Mondrian's attempts. For the eminent scholar or the cultivated Arabist, however, some of these convolutions invoke the benediction of Mahomet, and they read: *Baraktou Mohammadin!* (Mohammed bless you!) It happens that the intertwined Kufic alphabet or the flowery Kufic complicates the reading so much that it becomes practically impossible to fathom, except for the initiated or the erudite; but the way of

%

writing employed by Charles Maurras, for example, offers to the layman indecipherable gibberish, which the printers of *Action française,* the French periodical, unfailingly composed into an editorial! Another point to be kept in mind is the extreme difficulty of calligraphy, or of any writing system, for that matter. Something else again are our so-called calligraphies which randomly and (let us even admit) with an occasional bit of luck present us with vertical, round, and hooked strokes, as well as bold and delicate effects—and all this without reference to any particular rules. As long as these writing systems do not express a language accessible to normally constituted men, we are stretching language unpardonably if we use the word *calligraphy* at all in these cases. And it is futile to imagine that one may find in the calligraphies of the Far East a foreshadowing of non-objective art or in those of the Arab world a precedent for our ultra-letterists.

Let us rather heed Wou Tchong-hong: "To consider calligraphy as an abstract art, to tear it from the culture wherein it finds its most beautiful expression and fit it into a constricting alliance with poetry or painting, is to disfigure it. It will only be at the price of betraying calligraphy if abstract painting—individualistic, anarchic, in revolt against all conventions and all traditions—dares to consider itself its heir." (Unpublished memoir on "Chinese Calligraphy and Abstract Painting in the West of Today.")

Even though we realize that writing infinitely multiplies both knowledge and ignorance, falsehood and truth, and that it also can create or maintain perfectly beautiful forms, we are far from knowing all that there is to know about it.

An unknown handwriting on an envelope immediately attracts our attention and excites us: it is as conversational, as ungrateful, or as promising as an unknown face. In other days, when only the professional scribes practiced writing, the style of a particular school, of a particular civilization, was more important than personal handwriting. Even though some specific styles still exist today—for instance, that of the teachers trained in the normal schools of the Third Republic or that of those society women in whose handwriting the *ductus* of the fashionable French convents is recognizable, e.g. Sacré-Coeur, Oiseaux, most individuals, no matter how inadequately educated, now have their own distinctive handwriting.

So now we can understand the origin, the progress, and the excesses of graphology, so glorified by Balzac in his *Théorie de la démarche*: "Then, it was proved to me that autograph collectors and those who claim to judge the character of men through their handwriting were superior people." As for me—and I hardly consider myself a "superman" — handwriting, nevertheless, speaks to me, attracts or repels me, at least as much as lips, eyes, voices, or gestures. I take it into consideration when I judge people.

Here are the observations attested to by those who have conducted the following experiment: children of five or six years of age were asked to classify specimens of examinations written by candidates for the baccalaureate degree. They were instructed: "Put the pretty ones here; the ugly ones, there; and the others, over there." Usually, the same results are obtained as when these papers are corrected by the teacher! The well-done examination papers correspond to the "pretty" ones; the low-grade papers correspond to the "ugly" ones; and the mass of mediocre papers correspond to the "others." Throughout my thirty years of teaching, as soon as I have received the examination papers, I have separated them into three piles, according to whether the handwriting and the arrangement please me, displease me, or appear mediocre to me. It has happened, but quite rarely, that I have afterwards had to shift a paper from one pile to another (after all, when one is playing a game of chance, there are always unexpected eventualities).

This experience has enabled me to appreciate the professor of philosophy who one day returned the compositions to his college class and announced the two best marks. One of the papers he had rated excellent because he had not understood it very well and, therefore, feared that he might not be doing justice to the student for a thought that the professor considered extremely difficult; the other student got the excellent mark because he had presented the teacher with "very pretty handwriting."

Businessmen react in much the same way when they ask job applicants to send them a handwritten letter. It is easy to imagine them transmitting these letters to a graphology service, such as the one which periodically puts an advertisement in the paper, and from which I shall choose this extract: "...and no matter what your experience with people has been, you cannot, in the few moments set aside for the interview, detect in the applicant those qualifications you expect from him or those faults which would make you reject him. Whereas our *Graphological Analysis* immediately lets you know the person you are dealing with."

Well, well! Such jumping to conclusions! Consider the handwriting of André Breton or of Raymond Guérin, in each case so regular, so beautifully controlled, so well ordered. It would certainly have to be a very clever person who could deduce from their handwriting that it was produced by two rebellious temperaments, in revolt against everything. Except for the green ink which he sometimes uses, there is nothing more "classic," to my mind, than a letter of André Breton. Now, in the name of orthodoxy, of reason, of asceticism, of will power, Roger Caillois has, for nearly a quarter of a century, been fighting surrealism. But, is there anything less orthodox, less ascetic, more "romantic" than the handwriting of this "classicist"? Well, then?

It is true that the French periodical of former years, the *Canard Enchaîné,* was justified when it printed the signature of Montherlant, the author of several great books and of several others which are insignificant today, as M. Moi ["I"] de Montherlant, a signature which the writer readily acknowledged; whereas, the signature of the modest recluse, the refined father of the still more refined Clara d'Ellébeuse, Francis Jammes, unquestionably exhibited in his flourishes an unbridled vanity and a haughtiness almost satanic. If I examine the signatures which I have kept since my childhood — on my identification cards, for instance—how can I deny that they correspond quite closely to the successive phases of my developing character or to the changes which I have imposed on it? I can observe the evolution from the somewhat ambitious ingeniousness already evident in me and in my very ornate and rather hypocritical signature when I was eighteen years old, to a new phase from the age of twenty to twenty-

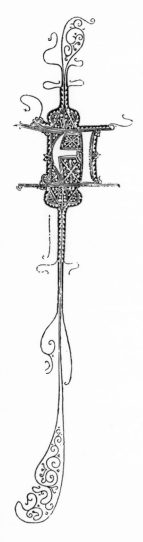

five years of age when my ambition became more sincere and was better applied—but how violent it was! It is not for me to judge my present signature.

Rather than a science, though, graphology appears to me to be an art: closer to medicine, and especially psychiatry, than to chemistry or mathematics. If the methods of intuitive graphology are relied upon, or those of analytical graphology (Crépieux Jamin), the chances for error are serious; that is, if one wishes to go beyond a general impression: sympathetic or antipathetic? strong-willed or weak-willed? intelligent or otherwise? loyal or hypocritical? sensitive or insensitive to beauty? ill or in good health? stingy or generous? As soon as a graphology expert tries to go beyond this point, he is vulnerable to ludicrous or grave errors. If a graphologist dates the texts of Rimbaud as if at random, as M. de Bouillane de Lacoste has done, only a slight error has been committed, one without serious consequences; but if, in a courtroom, the same so-called handwriting expert attributes to the accused a compromising document and the lawyers of the accused know and luckily can produce the real author, this business is no longer a laughing matter but smacks of a situation too reminiscent for us of the Dreyfus case. Today, especially, police techniques make it possible to use elements selected from someone's handwriting, to fabricate documents for the conviction of anyone whom it is desired to find guilty, even though the victim has never written this document. In such a case, graphology is an excellent way of convicting the innocent.

Used with discretion in normal and pathological psychology, however, graphology can help to complete a diagnosis. From merely looking at the handwriting of our friends, we all know how to recognize those whose disposition makes life dangerous. I knew a young man of extreme (even of exceptional) intelligence who was incapable of writing a single word of French correctly. After a long medical investigation, it was found that a rare mental quirk, which is, in fact, physiological, had made it a torment for him to write from left to right. I advised his family to make him study one of the Semitic languages, which are written from right to left. This time the spelling was assimilated without difficulty. It is established practice to use the drawings of the sick either to establish a diagnosis or to encourage a cure. Psychiatrists, then, should not, nor do they, neglect the help furnished by the handwriting of their patients.

The question arises: is it possible to go further and deduce from a script knowledge bearing on the psychology of the great masses of people? It must, of course, be understood that I am not referring here to those peculiarities which may be learned in school. I can identify a Pole merely by his *w*, even if he writes for me in faultless French; a subject of Her Gracious Majesty by his capital *t*; the young German by various other signs, even when he does not use the *Spitzschrift*. No. I mean: is a script capable of *informing* a civilization, in the literal sense of the word— *give form to something?* The Centre International de Synthèse arranged a seminar in Paris from May 3-11, 1960, on "l'Ecriture et la psychologie des peuples," writing and the psychology of people. "Since the handwriting of an individual reveals the idiosyncrasies of the writer, the writing of nations ought to reveal in some measure the peculiarities of the collective spirit of peoples," writes Marcel

Cohen in *"La grande invention de l'écriture et son évolution,"* the great invention of writing and its evolution.

Occupied by business in Poland, I was not able to be present at the Congress, and the papers read there had not as yet been published at the time of my writing this book. Nevertheless, I am aware of some of the ideas in the theses propounded there. Some experts consider that the writing material and the writing tool play decisive roles in the formation of scripts; others, and particularly Filliozat, think that writing makes many characteristics of mass psychology incontestably evident. In handwriting studies of several societies he described the very characteristics which helped him to determine even the costumes of the people. All the works of man are, in fact, interdependent: the art of gardening and of poetry; music and the dance; architecture and writing.

In choosing to abandon the Arabic alphabet in which the words of God are written, and to adopt the Latin alphabet, Kemal Ataturk affirmed his desire to secularize Turkey. The new script, which was a striking characteristic of the revolution, assured the success of the reforms. The proof *a contrario* is furnished us by the Aramaic script and also by the Greek. Both of these obstinately perpetuated themselves so that they could be used as weapons against colonizing forces and as a means of displaying fidelity to this or that religion. As for China, it is not necessary to follow Georges Margouliès to the end of his essay on "La langue et l'écriture chinoises," Chinese language and writing, to get his point. Of the 272 pages which comprise the first edition of this clever book (1943), eighty study the influence of writing on Chinese culture; thirty-five others set forth a parallel between Chinese and Western writing systems. The thesis is ingenious and radical: literature, philosophy, psychology, political and social organization—all of China is in her written characters.

The Indo-European languages, broken up into literal alphabetic signs, shape themselves into words which can only be obtained by a progressive synthesis of letters and syllables, the purpose of which is to be understood; these words do not have an existence of their own, subject as they always are to the changes of their endings, the alternation of vowels, and the conjugations (I go, we went, I have gone). The Chinese language, however, has as its base, the ideogram; that is, the word, stated once and for all—for all the cases, all the genders, all the tenses, all the persons and numbers, all the forms; the word, not in its auditory but in its visual form, only the design of which gives information as to the group of ideas to which it belongs.

To objective and abstract Chinese, which is perfectly adapted to the expression of thoughts, Margouliès opposes the languages of the West, which are always concrete and subjective. To the prolixity of dialects, he opposes the precision of a language developed for the eye. To the particularity of sounds, he opposes the incontestable universality of the image. To the semantic confusion of the Western press, he opposes the discipline which Chinese scholars maintain over the use of key words which may be affected only by neologisms or derived meanings. In this way, changes can be effected in the characters.

Before he is able to write, every scholar must study syntax and vocabulary for a very long time, just as in former days among us milliners or dressmakers learned by fashion-

d

ing articles with esparto-grass and carpenters shaped brass into frames for the tops of carriages, besides handling the saw and various kinds of planes. One does not write in Chinese without having read many good authors; one also reads for other reasons: for instance, to become familiar with rhetoric, so that the spirit or essence in China is always linked to form. It is only through form that this spirit is made manifest. And that is not all. Having nothing in common with vulgar speech or familiar language, the art of writing cannot be judged according to the laws of the spoken word. Every Chinese almost instinctively knows, having learned it for such a long time, that a good lecture is, perforce, a bad article, that beautiful discourse is *ipso facto* a dull piece of writing. Today, when our literature tends toward a journalistic style or is like a stenographic dialogue, we would do well to relearn these fundamental truths. There is this point to think about, too: the way we are going, our children won't understand us any more; every thirty years, our language will die. But in China, because of the character, there is no risk of obsolescence: the form of the *Li Sao,* or that of the *Li Ki* is more clear to literate people, after more than 2000 years, than the style of François Villon is to a Frenchman today or the style of Carlyle or Henry James to the Americans. Because of its continuity, literary tradition assures Chinese taste against instability, childishness, and intemperance.

The nature of the language has this additional curious effect: the art of writing is more literary than ours, and yet it is only in China that it may rightly be said: *ut pictura poesis, ut musica poesis.* This is because certain characters are an image for the eye, a little tableau of the object signified.

That the political, and especially the administrative, structure in China, on the other hand, may be explained *in part* by the use of characters, no one can deny. In agreement here with Margouliès, Jacques Gernet explains that it was the prestige and function of writing which account for "that particular institution of the Chinese world," the mandarinate. "Chinese functionaries considered themselves primarily men of letters, calligraphers, men skillful at literary composition and in the choice of efficient and useful new names, or rather, signs. Because of the practical virtues of writing, its function was conceived in China as a means of governing; the political activity was, from our viewpoint, certainly, an astonishing mixture of ritual, religious, and administrative acts." However, competitive examinations—a system inspired by the Chinese and transmitted by the Jesuits to France—function successfully not only in France, but in the Civil Service recruiting systems of England and the United States. This proves to me that those who explain the mandarinate system in China by citing the nature of the Chinese language exaggerate since it should be noted that the Indo-European languages of the Western countries with competitive examinations are alphabetical and not ideographic, like the Chinese.

In the domain of manners, morality, or religion, the ideas of Margouliès seem to be rather adventurous, though attractive. If morality were something "absolute," if history "ignores chance," one could accept the conclusions of this essay. But morality is relative and history is a tissue of fortuitous events. Therefore, it is better to listen to Jacques Gernet in his *Aspects et fonctions psychologiques de l'écriture en Chine,* psychological aspects and functions of writing in China. "It is evident that the psychological areas and aspects of writing are in close rapport with its functioning and with more or less restrained social groups who continued to use writing and were interested in its conservation." Between the end of the Chang dynasty and the seventh century B.C., writing was the privilege of schools of scribes and its "essential function was to permit, in the realm of divination and religious practices, a kind of communication with the world of gods and spirits. This fact points out the formidable power recognized to be inherent in writing and the respect mixed with mistrust which surrounded the writing specialists." From the Tcheou to Ts'in Che Houang Ti, the function of writing became secularized or was used to record the techniques of government: "It was probably at that time that distinctive forms of writing were developed in accordance with the different functions to which writing was put—cursive for the stenographic notation of the spoken word, seals for official writing, and the writing used on the stele..."

The rich character of Chinese writing also explains another fact of civilization: that the characters signifying happiness or longevity are reproduced in profusion on jewels, greeting cards, garments, furniture. Again quoting Jacques Gernet: "If written Chinese characters are used in this way, that is, for the expression of greetings, it is primarily so because of their specific form which corresponds uniquely to the reality which they are supposed to evoke; and, in the second place, because of their aesthetic value and ornamental function."

The nature of Chinese writing favored the origin and the persistence of a calligraphy inseparable from the art of the painter, and, in doing so, it considerably reduced the role of the spoken language to the level of poor relation. As each character accumulated a constantly growing mass of meanings and uses, the proliferation of these made it difficult to achieve a thorough knowledge of the classical Chinese language, this language which is called "written." Briefly, "the functions of pure communication" were developed in China "very much later than in the other civilizations" because these functions happened to be "in competition with others: ritualistic and aesthetic."

There is still a question to be taken up, a question which has been raised for some time by those who think about the future: will this or that script succeed some day in unifying the human race, or at least make less difficult that "communication of enlightenment" of which Leibnitz considered himself the champion?

Surely nothing is needed more today than a universal language. Would anyone involved in the study of science or engaged in some other serious discipline dare to consider himself well informed if he did not know what was being published about his subject in English, German, Russian, Italian, Spanish, French, Japanese? Tomorrow, he will again have to reckon with Arabic; after tomorrow, with Brazilian, Tamil, Hindi, Urdu, and so on. For example, in the field of Sinology, Poles and Hungarians have just produced works of the first order. Lacking translations, must we also learn Hungarian and Polish? Of course, it is easy to raise many arguments against each of the languages with universal pretentions; chauvinism is given free rein, and the most specious theories are used to justify strictly imperialistic ambitions. That is why the ad-

herents of Esperanto or of Arulo have not lost all hope, nor have those who favor Latin.

It is certainly less ambitious, but perhaps it is wiser to think about a universal writing system. Those who would let themselves be cut into pieces on the spot rather than to renounce their own language probably would accept modification of their writing system if they could discern in such action a commercial or cultural benefit. Any human group which seeks to unify itself politically must find a way of writing accessible to all the elements which it seeks to conciliate. Powerful though they were, the Pharaohs Amenophis III and Amenophis IV (1408-1354 B.C.), men whose own language was beautiful and whose empire was powerful, did not scorn to correspond in Sumero-Akkadian characters, that is, in cuneiform, with the Hittites and the sovereigns of Assyria, of Babylonia, of Mittani. If this was true, then, it is hard to imagine how our shrinking earth today can escape its destiny.

Already, it is impossible not to be aware of the diffusion of numbers called "Arabic," our numbers. Replacing Roman numerals which were hardly used in Italy except to note the years of the Mussolini era, not only have they conquered the Mediterranean world, but in Japan and China they are already often used to number the pages of books and as dates on coins. Even on the old silk route, in the middle of the Gobi Desert, I found that the information about distances carried on the new road signs is no longer indicated in Chinese characters, but in our numbers. This does not mean that there has been an overnight change or a sudden revolution; many Chinese books are still numbered according to the ancient system 十九八七六五四三二一

In the same way, our punctuation is in the process of conquering the world. Although the Chinese are still using for a period the sign belatedly introduced in their books ० and have ignored ours (.), they have borrowed the comma from us, as well as the semicolon, the sign indicating ellipsis, the question mark, the exclamation point, parentheses, and an equivalent of our quotation marks ⌐ ; and they have been influenced by our underlining to designate historical and geographical proper nouns (a fine sinusoid ∿∿∿ designating the titles of books). The Japanese turn our comma upside down, but employ it regularly; also they use our exclamation point and question mark, our ellipsis sign, an equivalent of our quotation marks ⌐ , and even our sigla, like *sqq.*, to indicate a pagination.

Although magazines and books printed in Arabic characters retain their numbers, this time really Arabic (and why should they surrender to their Christian adaptation?), the punctuation now follows ours. Sometimes, one simply transposes by using a mirror since Arabic is written from right to left. The comma, therefore, becomes ('), the semicolon (;), the question mark remaining as it is with us, as well as, of course, the period, the exclamation point, the dash, the colon, the ellipsis sign, the quotation marks, the parentheses, and the square brackets. In four centuries, French punctuation, conceived in the sixteenth century and subsequently perfected, has thus influenced the most remote languages. The evolution appears to be inevitable and irreversible, in view of the fact that we had perfected a system very much more elaborate than that of the peoples of Asia.

As for mathematical symbols, it was easier

for them to become universal because the so-called Arabic numbers stood side by side with Latin or Greek letters and even with certain signs from the Hebrew alphabet.

But what happens, what may one suppose will happen, to the great competing alphabets of today, notably those in which the languages of three powerful civilizations are written? Presumably, these civilizations desire to make their religions or ideologies universal. These three are: the Latin alphabet, language of Catholic and Protestant Christianity; the Arabic alphabet, vehicle of Islam; and, finally, the Cyrillic alphabet, which until 1949 considered itself to be the future of the socialist world.

In spite of some rumors of Latinization in the 1920's, and then again in 1933, the Cyrillic script has persisted, although it has been slightly simplified; Russian, Ukrainian, etc., are written in Cyrillic, but not the other languages of the Soviet Union, since the Congress of Baku instituted a "unified" alphabet, one which is adaptable to all the languages of the ancient Czarist Empire. Besides twenty-five Latin characters, called "fundamentals," seventy-two "secondary letters" were chosen and eight other signs as well, with the result that the Soviets have actually been able to notate exactly a language like that of the Abkhasians, which requires fifty-one signs, and that of the Ossetians, which needs only twenty-five letters. In doing this, the Communists ingeniously contributed to the diffusion of basic education and of Marxist-Leninist ideology. Proud of their old cultures, Armenians and Georgians have conserved their alphabets.

Because of the consonantal skeleton which determines them, the Semitic languages continue to resist Latinization, and even more so because two religions, the Jewish and the Moslem, strongly organize two of the peoples of this stock and intimately link writing to the religion. Although Arabic writing lost in Turkey to the Latin alphabet (the latter is much better adapted to the phoneticism of a Mongol dialect), it maintains itself in Shiitic Iran where the language, of Indo-European origin, would gain, more perhaps than Turkish, by Latinization. The vitality of the Arabic alphabet remains so great elsewhere that in Uzbekistan, where it is proscribed in principle, it is still alive in the Moslem calendars and even, as I am told, in everyday life where it is found in cursive form or shorthand. Every year in Black Africa, it goes hand in hand with the progress of Islam. But now that this continent is recovering its independence and is seeking links to its past, the influence of English, like that of French, will surely propagate the Latin alphabet, that of the old colonizers (English, Belgians, Spaniards, Frenchmen, Boers, Portuguese). The same phenomenon, then, will probably occur as in Indochina where three scripts are now used concurrently: Chinese characters, Chinese characters adapted to Vietnamese, and finally, the *quoc ngu*, a successful and living arrangement of the Latin alphabet. As another consequence of European colonialism, the Malayan languages have adopted our alphabet: in Madagascar, in conjunction with the efforts of French education, the influence of Catholic and Protestant missions favored the Latinization of Malagasy, while Dutch imperialism had the same effect in the Sunda Isles.

Without any Western prejudice whatsoever, then, it should be stated: the chances are that the legacy of the Phoenicians to the Greeks, to the Romans, and through them to Europe has a future before it.

As for India and Pakistan where languages abound, the unification of writing will be slow and difficult. Some Dravidian dialects there are written in scripts intended for languages of a heterogeneous type (Indo-European), while certain Indo-European dialects are transcribed into Arabic characters which are not at all suitable for them. As long as India will not be able to promulgate its own edict of Villers-Cotterets and impose a dominant language (which would undoubtedly be Hindustani), no one can foretell what the future of writing will be on this subcontinent; the country is divided between Hindi (Indian characters, Sanskrit vocabulary) and Urdu (Arabic characters, Islam).

With a script in which Chinese characters are mingled with the phonetic values of *kana* (and the more numerous the Chinese characters, the more scientific the language), Japan has demonstrated since the Meiji that a script alien to the Roman alphabet has never prevented anyone from rising to top rank in the hierarchy of knowledge and efficiency. Japan is certainly not considering abandoning its script, which could easily be Latinized because it enjoys, along with the other characters, its own polysyllabism.

On the other hand, since the revolution which brought the Communists to power in China, a great quarrel has been stirring. Opposing each other, on the one hand, are the followers of Zhdanov and the leftists (enemies of the characters and partisans of a radical Latinization of Chinese) and, on the other hand, the more thoughtful elements who wisely reason that, in renouncing ideograms, China would risk cutting herself off from her past. Of all the problems which writing poses for men at the present time, here surely is the one richest in consequences. According to whether it is solved in one way or another, men will or will not have the opportunity, at last, of having at their disposal a script truly capable of becoming universal.

The idea is not new. Hardly had he become acquainted with Chinese script, than Leibnitz with a stroke of genius understood that here was a universal script par excellence: "ex. gr. posset character Chinensis quem τὰ (*sic,* that is to say 大, *ta*) legunt, ab omnibus populis agnosci pro indicio magnitudinis, licet diversa in omnibus populis ejus foret lectio. Chinensis enim legeret τὰ, Graecus μέγας, Romanus *magnus,* Germanus *gross,* etc." (VI, 2a, p. 135). In English: "It is thus possible to take as the sign for "bigness" the character which the Chinese read *ta* 大, and this can be done in all nations, however diverse the pronunciation of this word might be. What the Chinese would pronounce *ta* 大, the Greek would pronounce μέγας, the Latin *magnus,* the German *gross,*" the French *grand,* etc. Nobody can actually contest this characteristic, peculiar to the Chinese: it is an "Esperanto for the eyes," according to the remark of the Swedish Sinologist Karlgren. Georges Margouliès agrees. For him, the only way to render any language, if not entirely clear, at least perfectly comprehensible in its constituent elements formed by the vocabulary, is to use a script which renders the meaning of words instead of the sound; that is, "ideographic writing."

The same advice had already been given by the Jesuit Kircher who, in his time, was capable of the worst follies (such as his belief in the derivation of the Chinese ideograms from Egyptian hieroglyphics, which he interpreted without rhyme or reason), but Kircher was also capable of the most audacious ideas. For him, Chinese writing among the Japanese, Koreans, Tonkinese (North Viet Nam) and Cochin Chinese (South Viet Nam) played a role equivalent to that played among us by algebra and arithmetic "which is understood by everyone even though the words which are used to explain them are different."

Vendryès, who did not understand Chinese, hurled unmerited reproaches at it: "There are, however, elementary grammatical ideas which ideographic writing does not render naturally; for instance, the distinction between the individual and the species, between the noun and the verb, tense, mood, the negative, etc.," reservations which could apply—if one insists upon this—to the *wen yen,* but not at all to the *pai-houa,* which is written in ideograms. Nevertheless, Vendryès recognized in Chinese writing the advantage "of being able to be read by people speaking different languages," in much the same way as the naval signal code. When the question of a universal script is debated, does not this advantage outweigh all the disadvantages?

In fact, what exactly are the disadvantages? When I hear it said, for example, that the Chinese *alphabet* (sic) has eighty thousand *letters* (sic), I am no longer surprised at the expression of so much prejudice against Chinese script! We should speak instead of the number of characters. Here, we nurture another myth: the forty thousand characters in the *Dictionary of K'ang Hi* must all be understood if one is to be literate! Actually, of the forty thousand characters listed there, four thousand are no longer in current usage; two thousand designate proper nouns or rare terms; thirty-four thousand constitute aber-

rant ways of writing which have no use except for the scholarly specialist. With about two thousand five hundred characters, journals, magazines, and novels of Communist China can be read fluently. Who says that an entire lifetime is needed to learn those signs? Don't we know young Frenchmen who, after five years of Chinese, two or three of them spent in China, not only speak Chinese fluently, but know and use many more than two thousand five hundred characters? If Chinese, then, is not to furnish humanity with the universal script which it sorely needs, it will not, in any case, be because this script lacks the required qualifications. Also, it would be advisable for the Chinese themselves not to substitute for their characters a Latinization which would only make of their written language the equivalent of Latin and Greek for us. According to the latest reports, it appears that the partisans dedicated to the conservation of the characters have temporarily won the difficult game they are playing against the leftists.

"There remains a problem in which none of us is disinterested, that of the future of Chinese characters. We are all convinced that, as a system of writing, they constitute an immortal contribution to our history. Will they remain intact permanently; will they change from their original forms; or will they be replaced by a phonetic language, whether in Latin letters or in some other phonetic script? It is not necessary to come to a hasty conclusion. Any language is destined to change, anyway, as changes in the characters have proved in the past. There will be changes in the future. We may also say that the day will come when the written or spoken languages of the different peoples of the world will gradually become one and the same language. The languages of humanity tend to approach one another gradually until, finally, no important differences will remain. To say this is to be optimistic, not pessimistic. As for knowing which system will be adopted, it is too soon to conjecture. On the question of the future of Chinese characters, views may differ and we can discuss them." (Chou En-lai.)

On the other hand, the commission charged by the Chinese government to reform writing, and whose secretary I saw in Peiping in 1957, told us unhesitatingly that "Chinese characters are eternal"; he meant that they will endure as long as Chinese civilization itself. If so, and I hope so, Chinese ideograms will be in a better position to furnish man with his universal script as the time approaches, if things evolve as one can foresee they may, when one man in three will be Chinese.

I am aware of the fact that most people in the West wish, and consequently hope, that the Latin alphabet will win over the Chinese characters. But since the universal script is going to favor "the diffusion of a common civilization," we would be naive to forget that politics will have its part to play. Let us suppose that Chinese communism conquers the earth. Is it not obvious what the chances would be then for their "Esperanto for the eyes"? If capitalism, on the contrary, conquers, the Latin alphabet, which transmits its culture, would have the opportunity to spread everywhere. Assuming that the two systems

survive, I doubt whether either of them would consider being won over by the script of the other! Those will be great days for the script-makers!

On this latter hypothesis, why shouldn't humanity adopt the alphabet developed by the International Phonetic Association, a complete alphabet capable of indicating all the phonemes or articulated sounds used in the world? Each language could then use those symbols which are indispensable to it. Everybody could easily learn even those letters not needed for the notation of their own language. Others dream, on the contrary, of a "simplified" alphabet. If I am to believe a piece of news which appeared in *Lettres françaises* (January 7-13, 1960), the executor of Bernard Shaw's will has just awarded a prize of 8,300 pounds sterling to four people chosen from among 467 candidates who have been laboring to simplify the alphabet and who are said to have reduced it "by twenty-three characters"! I take a dim view of a method of notating any language whatsoever with three letters!

Obviously false though this story must be, it is necessary to report it here if only to show that if one must go that far, why not return at once to the ideogram and, with Raymond Queneau, tell a story in Eskimo-style, inspired by those road signs which, in the middle of the twentieth century, lead us back to the origins of writing, while at the same time presaging a type of writing truly universal?

PHOTO CREDITS